CW00449658

The Empath

Awakening

By

Diane Kathrine

The Empath Awakening 2016

Contents

The Awakening

With the first stirrings of an Empath's awakening the seeds of transformation are sewn. The Empath rouses to a world in which they no longer feel well-versed. Everything seems different. They feel sensitive, open and vulnerable to their environment and an overwhelming awareness has developed.

Although always sensitive, the Empath now feels more susceptible to the energy of others and they are aware of so much more than they ever were.

The Awakening Begins

Awakening as an Empath thrusts you on an incredible journey that will see you expose many fascinating truths about yourself. Finally having an explanation for all you feel, experience and know, comes with a great sense of relief. You are not the only one. Those unusual traits of your personality, you saw as being oddities or insecurities, are part and parcel of being Sensitive. The awakened Empath also comes to recognize that it's a Sensitivity not many others know of or appreciate.

The need to understand your "strange" life experiences is what brought you towards the Empath awakening, to the unearthing of your unusual gift, and the abilities that go with it.

What does the start of this astonishing new journey look like? For most it will mean questions, lots and lots of questions.

The search for Empath secrets and knowledge will take you on a new path. It is a route unfamiliar to the wayside previously encountered and a winding road that knows no boundaries. As an Empath you have always been on the lookout for answers, even if you are not aware of it. But when you know the direction in which to travel, your journey becomes easier.

What the Empath Awakening Looks Like:

- **Feeling sensitive and open:** The first signs of the awakening comes with a sharpened sense of external energy. The Empath feels overly sensitive and vulnerable to the energy of others, which often gives rise to emotional pain and insecurities.

- **Spending time in public places is overwhelming:** When they awaken the Empath become more susceptible to the emotional energy of others. Busy peopled places, like shopping malls, supermarkets or stadiums, feel unpleasant to the newly awakened.

- **Experiencing other people's emotions and mistaking them for one's own:** Some will feel emotions off those nearby, others from those a distance away, or both. Picking up emotions and claiming ownership of them is a common theme in the newly awakened. It can take some time to learn to differentiate between one's own emotions and those of others.

- **Acute intolerance of negativity:** Anyone who behaves in a negative manner becomes toxic to the Empath. As their vibration rises it becomes more challenging to be around those who show a lack of enthusiasm towards life. Even watching TV or reading papers, where there is violence or misery, becomes intolerable.

- **Digestive disorders and lower back problems:** The solar-plexus chakra, situated in the center of the abdomen, is known as the seat of emotions. This is where Empaths feel the energy of others which, can weaken the area and eventually lead to stomach troubles. Lower back problems develop from being ungrounded (amongst other things) and one who has no knowledge of being an Empath, will almost always be ungrounded.

- **Empath fatigue:** Empaths regularly feel drained and fatigued, either from spending too much time around energy-draining-people, picking energy up from others, or being overstimulated. This type of fatigue is not cured by sleep or rest.

- **Sudden desire to learn about metaphysical subjects and healing:** Empaths are often born healers. When they awaken a desire to become more knowledgeable develops. Anything of a supernatural nature is of interest to an Empath. They don't surprise or get shocked easily, even at the revelation of what others would consider unthinkable.

- **Need for solitude:** Spending periods of time sitting alone in silence becomes the norm for the Empath, and a much needed respite, necessary to rebalance and recharge. The Empath becomes overstimulated if they don't get quiet time.

- **Avoids what they don't enjoy**: When the Empath awakens they begin to reach for the truth. Their lives and desires change. Doing jobs or social activities they don't enjoy is no longer bearable.

- **Weight gain:** Sensitivity stress, from picking up energy off others, can lead to an excess of cortisol, which often develops into belly fat. As Empaths are often drawn to sugar and carbohydrate-rich foods, to cope with emotional residuals and as a quick-fix of energy, they are more prone to carrying weight. These foods create an excess of glucose in the bloodstream which, if not used for energy, is stored as fat.

- **Intolerance to bad behavior and narcissism:** Although kind and tolerant of others, awakened Empaths do not like to be around overly egotistical people, who put themselves first and refuse to consider anyone's feelings or points of view other than their own.

- **Sudden aversion to meat:** The more Sensitive the Empath becomes, the more they sense the energy in their food. They often turn away from meat or poultry because they can feel the vibrations of the animal, especially if the animal suffered. Low-energy food triggers low emotional energy.

- **A Desire to be invisible to others:** Empaths are prone to mood swings. If they've taken on too much negative energy, they will appear quiet or even miserable. When overloaded they have little energy to give to others. But, being good listeners, people like to offload their problems and the Empath dutifully listens. Sometimes it is easier not to be seen than to turn one away who wants to unburden themselves.

- **A sudden increase in intuition and psychic abilities:** The Empath always had strong intuition but upon awakening it kicks up another gear, as do other synchronistic events and strange random occurrences.

- **Hypersensitive to certain people:** There is often a shift in the sociable nature of an awakened Empath, no longer being able to abide spending time with certain friends, family members or colleagues. Or an inability to tolerate those they formerly had close relationships with, develops.

- **A Stronger Connection to Nature**: It is when they spend time in nature, the Empath becomes centered. The newly awakened find themselves drawn to the great outdoors, without necessarily understanding why, and will make more of an effort to spend time in the natural world.

  Whether you are new to learning you are an Empath, or if you have known for many years, I do not need to tell you this is a challenging path to walk. Nor do I need tell you that armored with the knowledge of who you are, life will suddenly become a breeze… sadly, that's not the way it works.

  Empath life is not just a way of being, it is a life purpose, a gift, a trial, an initiation, and a chance to better oneself and rise above the challenges of living in a world based on manipulation and deceit.

Each decade of Empath life uncovers more mysteries and tests to unravel and complete. To be able to compete in these trials we first have to work at finding Empath balance. We cannot think of making any waves in life if we are taken down by our Sensitivities and/or poisoned by toxic energy and people. It does not have to be this way. We should not have to hide from the world because of the way it makes us feel.

If willing to keep working towards change, you will come to understand your hidden knowledge and power. Your life, and all that you feel, will then make sense and you will discover your true purpose. And you know what? it really is worth the effort!

1

Being an Empath

One of the biggest hurdles an Empath has to overcome, when awakening, is understanding where their imbalances lie.

For some, their weakness is buried within their body, others in their mind and emotions, but for most, their imbalances are etched deep into their energetic body and they will only find balance once the necessary adjustments are made.

When we allow our intuition, and deep inner Knowing, to guide us it will show us the changes we need to make towards a life of transformation. Finding this book is a step in that direction.

The challenges we face, in the early stages of Empath awakening, come about when we don't understand our ways. There are many complexities to being Sensitive which aren't discussed in our everyday life, in schools, families or places of work.

Empaths are enigmas and their ways often shrouded in mystery. Uncovering their truth can seem a daunting task, but it does not have to be.

It is said only 5 % of the global population are Empaths, but I suspect that number to be considerably higher.

Some people go through their whole life without discovering they are Sensitive and don't get to know what a rare and precious gift they possess. It is too easy to get caught up in the rat-race of life, and distracted from one's true purpose.

Life distractions explain why some don't learn the truth of who they are, or understand why they endure such tremendous emotional upheavals.

Many "unknowing" Empaths get so bogged down with the emotional trauma, that goes with being an unbalanced Sensitive, that they get no further than their GPs office in their quest for answers.

Being wrongly diagnosed with depression, or other mental disorders, is a common theme for an unaware and out-of-balance Empath. If medications are used to treat their "symptoms" it will just mask a deeper problem brought about by being energetically open and highly Sensitive.

There are many steps to take to make living in the world easier for the Empath. But, just like anything in life, what works for one does not always work for another.

Finding the best way to stay in balance proves to be a test for most, but having knowledge gives you power.

Learning simple ways of being will allow you to thrive, and not just survive, in the world. Giving you the ability to enjoy your gift instead of seeing it as a curse.

Before we look at ways to thrive in this world, it is a good idea to have a better understanding of some of the more dominant Empaths ways.

So, before we go any further we will take a brief look at traits which set the Empaths apart from others:

Certain People Cause Discomfort

These feelings are a caused by your Empathic antenna sensing something is not right in another's energy signature. It is triggered by you picking up a hidden agenda within their energy.

Whatever they are hiding, it will be a trait or emotional pain they do not want others to know about. Maybe they buried a part of their history they found too painful to face, or it could be a personality mannerism they dislike and want to keep masked, it could be inauthentic behaviour worn as camouflage, or you may be sensing a manipulative nature.

Whatever personality trait the other person is hiding, the Empath senses it as feelings of discomfort.

When an Empath comes across hidden emotional pain, inauthenticity or dark energy, within another, it is common for them to energetically shut down. This can be seen as stumbling over words, feeling mentally incapacitated with one's memory and thought process being affected, or becoming verbally frozen. The Empath is not consciously choosing these responses, it just happens. The contradictive energy of the other person scrambles their brain, making normal activities a challenge. This influence is worse in those who have a weakened or permeable aura (more on this later), both the Empath or the other person.

A weak aura creates a merging or clash of energy. To the Empath this feels like an energetic parasite has attached itself. The merging of energy creates too much mental data and this temporarily fries their circuits.

Dislikes Public Places

Train stations, shopping malls, stadiums or airports, where lots of people are around, can fill the Empath with a surge of random emotions that can be confusing and overwhelming. It is caused by a conflict of energy.

Empaths are energetically open and sense things most others don't even notice. When in peopled places, they often pick up a huge dose of emotions which come at them from all directions. As already noted, this will be felt more by those whose aura is weakened, meaning people's energy seeps into the Empath's energy-field and it causes chaos.

After getting "peopled" there is too much energy for the Empath to process and will lead to a big dose of fatigue, brain-frazzle and emotional overload.

When you start opening up as an Empath, it is not uncommon for these sensations to increase and, in some cases, become unbearable. If this happens it is highlighting the fact that you are either ungrounded or unbalanced and need to take protective measures before venturing out (lots of information here on how this can be done), or a phobia of public places may develop.

Encompasses Strong Intuition

Empaths know stuff without being told and have a heightened sixth-sense.

If something feels off to the Empath it will be.

The easiest way to see their intuition at work is on first impressions. When an Empath first meets anyone they unconsciously read their vibrations. Their intuition then tells them information about the person: whether they are trustworthy, an emotional match, or if they will likely cause them trouble.

Many brush off their intuitive encounters as coincidences. But by tuning into their intuition it can prevent the Empath from making poor life choices and guide them towards their true destiny.

Senses Residual Energy

History leaves an energetic imprint which Empaths can sense.

Happy, sad, angry or painful events leave potent residual energy. The more powerful the event, the more it is sensed by the Empath.

"Residual energy" is a term all Empaths become familiar with, it is often used when describing the energy remnants left in objects, places or buildings by the people who have gone before.

When a traumatic event has happened in an area, it leaves a powerful imprint within the energy which Empaths, and anyone who is Sensitive, can perceive. The same can be said if there has been a lot of anger, hate or erratic emotions within a particular place.

It may take a while for the Empath to recognize what they sense, in the form of residual energy, but once they understand it they can piece together some useful information and collect the back-story to many places, buildings and objects.

Easily Drained

Because an Empath unwittingly picks up the energy off others they can become over-stimulated when in social settings, even while spending time with friends or loved ones.

Being over-stimulated will lead to a drain in their energy and a dose of Empath fatigue.

Too much social stimuli can bring the Empath down for days, whether being at a party or spending an evening with close friends.

Owns a Creative Mind

From singing, acting, drawing or writing an Empath boasts a strong creative streak and a vivid imagination.

Work, school and home life have to be kept interesting and creative for an Empath, to keep them engaged and stimulated.

Empaths need to participate in some sort of creativity for their soul growth.

Creativity is a perfect way to free the mind and liberate the soul.

We live in a world governed by rules. Being creative allows for self-development and freethinking, it accesses your imagination, and is a chance to be innovative.

Innovation develops your brain and helps build intuitive awareness.

Creativity becomes a passport to self-discovery. Most people do not know their true-self, which causes great unhappiness.

When you express yourself creatively it opens up your mind and develops a natural curiosity for life. This in turn puts you on the path to finding your truth.

Any Empath who does not express herself creatively will feel trapped and uninspired towards life. By looking for ways to be creative it will serve as an energetic outlet and releases freethinking.

Keen Observer

Many Empaths don't realize they own this trait because they assume everyone has keen observational skills.

Empaths notice a change in people's moods, a shift in the vibration of someone's voice when they are uncomfortable; a flicker of an eye that shows another has been incensed or an inconsistency in a story.

The Empath can walk into a room and see many things others don't: a picture off center, dust on a blind, someone behaving out of character, an excitable vibe or low mood.

When the Empath embarks on their journey of self-discovery, and makes changes to balance and evolve, they notice even more: Colours become more vibrant, aromas more fragrant, music more empowering and nature more marvellous and fascinating.

The Ability to Read Others

Being able to read another is effortless for the Empath. It is like cold reading except most Empaths don't do it on purpose, an awareness just comes to them in regards to another.

Voice vibrations and micro-movements are also revealing to the Empath; they receive information about people without looking for it.

If someone is saying one thing whilst thinking another, the Empath picks up on this as contradictive energy.

In the early days, it may feel like we are judging others, when information comes to us, but we are actually unconsciously reading them.

Many Empaths scan the energy of others without realizing they are doing it. Scanning is an inbuilt form of protection. When scanning, we are doing it as a way to gauge whether we are safe to trust a certain other. But because many Empaths are not aware of this ability, they ignore the intuitive observations they receive.

A Good Listener

Empaths are born listeners. Listening comes as naturally as breathing. The downside to regularly lending an ear means we may become a dumping ground for everyone else's problems. If we are not vigilante, whilst listening to others' woes, it is guaranteed their problems will become our own.

Empaths genuinely listen and hear what others have to say. Because this is rare in today's society, it can become like a drug to those who want to be heard or love to talk about themselves.

Taking on other people's troubles, as well as dealing with their own, can make life difficult for the Empath. For this reason, many close themselves off, mentally, in an attempt to detach from those who bring them down.

Hypersensitive

Empaths are often told they are overly sensitive and take things too personally. Being sensitive goes hand in hand with being an Empath and cannot be changed. That said, our sensitivities are greatly heightened by being out-of-balance. Criticism then cuts deeper, emotional pain is more exaggerated and disloyalty or rejection, devastating.

Empaths feel everything deeply but when out of alignment all adverse emotive sensations become overstated and tormenting.

Not understanding why people don't feel or think the same way can be confusing.

Often going out of their way not to inconvenience or hurt others, in many case putting others needs first, Empaths are wounded by those who do not show the same courtesy. It takes time for an Empath to realize that much of the populace has only a fraction of their compassion and consideration.

Because an Empath's empathy and sensitivity is hardwired, they know no other way. If someone, they care about, lets them down or acts inconsiderately, it will wound the Empath deeply. Because they have such strong empathy it is hard for them to rationalize with those who don't.

Once balanced, the Empath can train themselves to change the way they react to disappointments and let-downs. They will not stop feeling, but their level of sensitivity will be drastically toned down.

Perceives Emotions in Others

The Empath perceives emotional energy off people, from both near and afar, but it may take time for them to make the connection of what they are enduring. This emotional energy is difficult to distinguish from their own and leaves many Empaths confused.

Just because an Empath senses another's anguish does not mean they automatically understand what it signifies or why it affects them so negatively.

Unfamiliar emotional energy leaves the unaware and unbalanced Empath ungrounded. Recognizing the origin, and understanding its impact, reduces the undesirable impression some foreign energy leaves. We gain this recognition by building our awareness, intuition, and by finding equilibrium.

Until we find balance, we need to know how to protect ourselves from any wayward energy, that may present itself.

Has an Addictive Nature

Alcohol, drugs, sugars and starchy carbohydrates are just some of the vices an Empath may binge on and hide themselves behind. Overindulging, in these addictions, is a way to block out external energy and subdue their inner-turmoil. But, what most don't realize, these vices actually enhance emotional turbulence rather than supress it.

Part of the road to Empath empowerment involves breaking away from any addictive patterns and the consumption of mind/mood altering substances. An Empath will never be free until they are free from that which keeps them imprisoned... any type of addiction!

Addictions are not just related to food and drink. We acquire addictive behaviours without realizing: Obsessive compulsive disorder OCD, a need for perfection, over analysing the behaviour of others, thinking too much, overdoing exercise, gorging on victim mentality, or having the need to please others, are just a sampling of ways that are part of an addictive nature. There are many more.

If we fail to spot our addictions, or allow them to go left unchecked, they will consume us and prevent us from finding oneness.

Embodies Physical Symptoms of Others

Not only will an Empath feel other peoples' emotional pain, and take it on as their own, they can also develop the ailments off others.

Irritations, disorders and body aches can appear like sympathy pains. An out-of-balance Empath need only briefly be in the presence of someone with a slight sniffle to pick up a full-blown dose. Of which, the ensuing symptoms are often worse than those of the original carrier. This is due to the Empath being highly open to the suggestions of other people's energy. Being influenced by other people's aches, pains and maladies is greatly reduced when the Empath finds balance. They may still feel the physical discomforts, of those suffering, but won't embody their symptoms or take them on as their own.

Abhors Narcissism

Although kind and tolerant of others, Empaths dislike to be around overly egotistical people or narcissistic types. Those who put themselves first and refuse to consider anyone's feelings, or points of view, other than their own will deflate an Empath's energy. In some cases, this repugnance has been garnered after being burnt by a narcissist.

There is often a toxic-like draw/divide, or love/hate relationship, between the Empath and the narcissist.

Most will have had a bad experience with one at some point in their life.

An Empath may try to fix the narcissist, in what they see as being broken, but it will often result in the Empath being broken for their efforts.

Possesses Heightened Senses

We are all sensory beings, meaning we can regulate certain data through our given senses: sight, sound, taste, touch and smell. In those who are Sensitive, these senses are heightened.

Sounds may be louder and more uncomfortable to the Empath. They can become easily irritated by loud noise or sudden bangs, especially within quiet places. Their vision is vivid, with colours appearing brighter and more luminously.

The Empath's sense of smell is often keen and amplified. Certain aromas, which others may not notice, can create an overwhelming repulsion. Being in the presence of someone wearing a strong scent or standing near one with poor hygiene, can literally turn the Empath's stomach.

The Strongest Trait

The strongest trait of an Empath is taking on the energy and emotions of other people. These people do not have to be connected, in any way, for them to have an effect. Simply sitting next to someone on a bus can mean you take home their personal issues.

The aim of this book is to help the Empath recognize their traits, imbalances and weakness and then work to overcome them, so they become the Empowered Empath they were born to be. It is possible!

2

Unite the Trinity

The biggest steps the Empath can take towards a happy, healthy life is by balancing the trinity of mind, body and spirit.

If you follow my blog, or have read any of my books, you will notice I talk a lot about stabilizing the trinity: for good reason. All three are connected and when one is out-of-balance so becomes the rest.

Discovering where the problem lies within the trinity, fixing the damage and making necessary changes, creates unity. If you want to become empowered as an Empath this is the only way.

The mind is our thoughts, ego and emotions. The body our physical vessel. And the spirit is our invisible self, comprising of our soul, aura and energy centers (chakras). We are all different. Each exceptional in our mind, body and spirit and, when it comes to re-balancing, we need to discover for ourselves what works to heal and stabilize.

We are as unique and brilliant as a beautiful snowflake. Being so singular and special, our imbalances can prove to be the same. Some people need speeding up, some slowing down, some will benefit from a high protein diet, some a high-carbohydrate diet, some need to get out of their heads, some need to get inside their heads, some need routine and rules and others space and freedom.

Because of our own diversity, the path for us to connect our mind, body and spirit is exclusive to us.

When the trinity is in turmoil, energetic imbalances create a repetitive cycle of damage: the mind weakening the body, the body weakening the spirit and the spirit weakening the mind.

If the Empath strives for unity, even before problems occur, it will keep them in a high vibrating space and prevent this repetitive cycle. Prevention is better than cure.

The trinity can become unhinged by any one, or several, of the following factors: poor diet, lack of exercise, chakra misalignment, getting peopled, spiritual awakening, a permeated aura, Sensitivity stress, hormonal imbalance, an overactive mind, drugs, alcohol, caffeine, chemicals and preservatives, allergies, food intolerances, prescriptive medications, GMOs, refined and processed foods, energy overload, spending too much time around negative, draining or damaging people, Empath fatigue, and imbalance in the part of the brain responsible for emotions (amygdala and insular cortex), and many more.

As Empaths, we often notice it is after spending time with others when we get overwhelmed or cast into emotional disarray.

Empaths pick up the energy of others and, even when in balance, are influenced by its charge. Problems arise when unfamiliar energy creates an overload which, if it happens on a regular basis, eventually leads to problems.

People-related-energy-issues worsen over time and become severe if left unchecked.

Let's take a look at how an imbalance of the mind, body and spirit occurs in three very different Empaths, and how it impacts their life:

Jane

Jane is a happy-go-lucky Empath, who works in a small bookshop in her local village and loves her job. She is a vegetarian, practices yoga three times a week and meditates every day. She adores socializing and going to the cinema.

When she was a teenager Jane used to be slim but over the years her weight has slowly crept up. Since hitting her thirties, Jane has become very overweight. She enjoys her food and eats lots of bread and pasta. To counteract her weight problem, she decided to go on a diet.

In her bid to lose weight, Jane started eating low-fat and low-calorie processed foods. Little did she know that these foods had a minimum nutritional content and were filled with chemicals and preservatives.

Jane lost weight quickly but she always felt tired, hungry and in a grumpy mood. People would comment on how great she looked, since she lost her weight, and this kept her resolve to stick with her diet.

After a year, Jane had lost enough weight and decided to ditch the diet. Before long, she found herself putting weight back on, despite the fact she was still drinking diet sodas and eating low-fat foods.

In recent times, Jane had also noticed when out in public places she was picking up the energy of others more intensely, which wiped her out and affected her moods for days. Jane had always felt other people's emotional energy, but now it felt like she was taking on these emotions as her own. Over time this got worse and Jane found herself becoming more depressed and reclusive. If she spent time with anyone who had the slightest air of negativity, hostility or pained emotions, it literally fried her circuits.

Jane stopped enjoying life, she was overweight, highly sensitive to the energy of others, depressed and emotional... What happened...?

Although Jane's diet was poor, she made it worse when she went on a diet. The foods she ate held no nutritional value and were damaging to her body.

She was literally starving herself with empty food. Her body may have looked better and slimmer, but inside it was damaged and unhealthy.

By unbalancing her hormones, her diet affected her mind as well as her body. Jane started putting weight back on, which added to her health issues, and because she continued to eat nutritionally devoid foods containing wheat, aspartame, refined sugar, trans-fats, GMOs, MSG, and other chemical nasties, her energetic signature altered.

Jane's vibration was low, her aura became permeable and she picked up the energy of others whenever she went out, which made her more depressed. There was a trinity imbalance which needing fixing.

We will look at how Jane can rebalance shortly, but first let's take a look at John:

John

John is also an Empath, although he was not aware of it. He works in the city in a high powered, stressful job. John eats a healthy organic diet and keeps fit by indulging in competitive sports.

John is very good at his job and enjoys it. At work he was social and confident but deep down this is not the way he felt inside. Everyone assumes John is an extrovert, when he is in fact the opposite. John puts on a bravado at work and plays the role well. He socializes after work with his colleagues but always needs alcohol to help him feel comfortable.

When he was in his twenties, John had no problem faking his personality, but now in his mid-thirties, it is becoming harder to do. Also, the stress of his job is getting to him, he can't sleep at night and cannot switch off from his to-do-list.

Even taking part in his sporting pastimes offers no respite. John's stress levels get worse. He starts suffering with intense stomach pain and gets diagnosed with a stomach ulcer. He is put on powerful acid blocking medication, which has the side-effect of making him constipated. To counteract the constipation, he also has to take daily laxatives.

John starts to notice he cannot spend time in certain people's company without being drained. Those in the office who have big egos or narcissistic types make him feel anxious or angry.

When he goes out socially, John needs to drink many beers to block out what he is picking up from colleagues and others in the bar. John finds himself getting more depressed, fearful and tired. He gets so fatigued that he cannot do his job properly.

He takes time off sick and finds himself becoming reclusive, he doesn't even like answering the phone. John does not want to connect with anyone because every time he does he becomes overwhelmed by their energy. He misses his job and wishes he could regain some kind of normalcy in his life... What happened?

Although John coped with his stressful job in his twenties, the stress was gradually weakening his body. Once he got to the age of thirty his body was less resilient, the stress did more damage and eventually caused a stomach ulcer.

By pretending to be gregarious and outgoing, when he was really an introvert, it drained his vital energy making him more vulnerable to stress. The worry that kept him awake at night, also affected his mind, and made his body produce too much adrenaline, which unbalanced his hormones and chakras. The medications John was taking had side-effects and further debilitated his body.

The imbalance in his body and mind caused a tear in his energy-field (aura) allowing more foreign energy in, which in turn created more stress. The negative Empath attributes kicked-in, making John's life difficult and pained.

Two different Empaths, with two very different lifestyles, both of whom are brought down by an imbalance in their mind, body and spirit. Jane's problems arose because of a poor diet, John's by stress. Now let's look at Eileen:

Eileen

Eileen is an Empath. She is in her late twenties. Is of normal weight and eats a reasonable diet. Eileen is quiet, but not shy, she likes to read and doesn't like socializing much, even though she has many friends. She works hard at her job as an events coordinator, and loves hiking.

Colleagues and friends love to come to Eileen to offload their problems or to ask her advice, but it always makes her feel weak after, as if she has taken on their problems or given a part of herself away. She can always tell when someone is lying, or not being their true-self, and she notices things most others don't. To the outside world Eileen seems like a lovely normal girl but her quiet demeanor disguises a deep hidden pain.

When Eileen was a teenager her father suddenly passed away. The grief was so overwhelming she did not know how to cope. Eileen decided to bury her pain. She never allowed herself to think about her father's death and never talked about it, or him, to anyone, not even her mother.

As she moved through her twenties, Eileen always felt sad inside, like her soul was unhappy. She lived under, what felt like, a grey cloud. But, despite this, she always had a smile and time for everyone. Apart from her inner-sadness, Jane still functioned in the world until, in her mid-twenties, when she started to suffer panic attacks. The attacks would get so intense that at times she did not want to leave her home. Eileen went to her doctor, who prescribed her with anti-depressants.

The anti-depressants helped a little with the panic attacks and made her feel less agitated, but Eileen still did not feel happy inside. She started to notice that everywhere she went she would feel uncomfortable when around people. If she went to the supermarket, and other shoppers got too close, she would feel waves of anger well up inside. If she spent too much time in public places, Eileen suffered with crushing fatigue and felt anxious. Even spending time with certain members of her family would make her experience undesirable emotions, which could last for days. She also became more defensive and sensitive to any kind of criticism.

Eileen tried avoiding all social situations but couldn't avoid people because of her job. Life became more difficult. Eileen started to feel like she would never find happiness, her moods fluctuated between being sad, flat or just ok. Life no longer made sense... What happened?

Because Eileen buried the pain of her father's passing, and did not process it, the pain remained and gradually built and did more and more damage within. She was like a ticking time-bomb.

Eileen's body had to find a way to release her inner-turmoil and get her attention as to how much damage it was doing. It was only a matter of time before she exploded, which happened in the form of panic attacks.

Because her father had passed away ten years ago, Eileen had no idea her panic attacks were linked to her grief. Because her doctor gave her anti-depressants, she assumed she was just depressed. The medication suppressed her pain a little, but did not release it. Eileen's buried pain became etched within her energy-field, which weakened and became permeable. Her leaky aura allowed too much energy in from others which overwhelmed her and added to her emotional burden, making it feel like she could never feel happiness.

Eileen's problems started by her repressing her grief, which went on to weakening her energy-field, then her body and mind.

Healing

As you can see. We have three Empaths with three very different lives and causes for imbalance. Now we will take a look at how each of them can find balance.

Jane

Jane is out-of-balance in her mind, body and spirit but the steps to re-alignment are different to John's and Eileen's. The place we start is by addressing what caused the initial problem.

She is prone to carrying weight and too much excess weight puts stress on the body. To lose weight healthily, and keep it off, Jane needs to remove wheat and refined sugar completely from her diet, both of which are addictive and encourage overeating, disrupt the natural flow of hormones, and affect brain chemistry. Jane needs to fill her diet with nutritious fruits and vegetables and healthy proteins such as nuts, seeds and tofu. Even though she is a vegetarian, Jane would benefit from including oily fish in her diet three times a week (if at least during the re-balancing stage).

Jane meditates and practices yoga, which is good, but she also needs to do some aerobic exercise, to burn energy (both her own and what she picks up) and help her shed more weight. By taking these steps, Jane's body will heal. This in turn will help repair her permeable aura and balance the mind, body and spirit.

After making the changes, Jane is now a happy balanced Empath and although she feels the emotional pain of others, no longer takes it on as her own.

John

The approach to John's realignment takes him on a different path to Jane.

John's problems started in his mind by being highly stressed, which then weakened his body causing an ulcer. To heal John, he needs to first address his stress response. John wants to return to his job in the city but he would like to be able to better cope with the stress that comes with it.

First, John must behave in a way which reflects his true personality and stop pretending to be someone he's not.

For thirty minutes each morning, before work, John must practice yoga and meditation. This ritual has the effect of preventing stress from doing damage, empowering and strengthening the body and building a stronger energy-field. It also gives him the confidence to be himself. If he needs time-out during the working day he should go to the bathroom, or any quiet place, and practice grounding exercises for five minutes.

Every evening, after work, John practices a muscle relaxation exercise, to rid any tension held in his muscles and body, before having a lavender salt bath. The salt, in the bath, will clear away any foreign energy, picked up from others, and the aroma of the lavender is instantly relaxing, clearing any stress and aiding in a good night's sleep. John also needs to stop drinking alcohol as it heightens stress and fearful emotions.

As he already eats a healthy diet John is advised to take zinc and vitamin C, to build up his immune strength, and a probiotic to rebalance the gut flora.

Following this advice, John is now a happy balanced Empath and, although he works in a high-powered job, is not brought down by the stress.

John still socializes with his colleagues, but only for a short period of time, and now drinks water instead of beer. He still does not enjoy being around negative, egotistical people but is always pleasant towards them, whilst avoiding spending time in their company.

Eileen

The path Eileen takes to rebalance, again, differs from both Jane and John.

On recommendation from a family member, Eileen visits a holistic grief counselor who helps with releasing her suppressed grief. She is also weaned off her anti-depressant medication.

Eileen has a series of reiki healing sessions, focused on her heart, which helps heal and release the deep sorrow accumulated there. In turn, the reiki helps strengthen and rebuilds her damaged energy shield.

Eileen takes up meditation, Dru yoga and Zumba classes. The meditation and yoga to still, strengthen and create flexibility in her body and mind, and the Zumba classes to put a sense of joy and fun, which had long since been missing, back into Eileen's life.

Within six months, Eileen finds joy has crept into her heart. The grief, she had held onto for so long, is no longer buried and, although she feels a pang of sadness every time she thinks of his passing, she can happily talk about her father with her family.

It was during her healing, Eileen discovered she is an Empath and that she is vulnerable to taking on other people's emotional energy. Eileen knows she will always have to remain vigilante of staying in balance and protected.

The changes that occurred for Eileen were so profound that she decided to train as a healer and holistic life coach, so she too could help others in the same situation.

The Moral of the Story

You can and will find happiness and harmony as an Empath.

Your gift does not and should not be seen as a curse. When you become stabilized and in control, you will be amazed at how your world transforms. Getting to the root of your troubles is where you need to start.

To get a better understanding of how imbalance occurs within the Empath, in either the mind, body and spirit, we will look at each one in turn...

3

Mind Over Matter

The mind is the super power within the trinity and encompasses more than just our thoughts and mental wellbeing. It is the place the ego likes to dominate and is the control center for our beliefs and opinions.

Our mind has a direct impact on our emotions, by the way of our thought patterns, and plays a huge part in the Empath's happiness.

When out-of-balance, the Empath mind triggers destructive thoughts which then lead to emotional stress.

If our thoughts and emotions are not in harmony, it unbalances our physical and energetic bodies. Not only will this lead to illness and instability, but it will likely impair our entire energy signature (spirit).

Empaths are known to have active imaginations and are deep thinkers.

Balanced, everyday thinking is healthy and productive, but over-zealous and repetitive thoughts, that are sticky and difficult to shake off, become problematic.

We have a 17 second window in which to engage or deny a thought. If we get caught off-guard, by a random low-level thought, we have a choice whether to connect to it, but the choice must be made within 17 seconds.

Once engaged, a dark thought can keep us stuck in our mind for hours. If our thoughts take a trip into the darker realms of opinion or resentment, then they will activate uncomfortable or damaging emotions.

If we pick up negative energy, from others, it can activate a lower tone of thinking and cloud our judgements, which also creates dark and repetitive thoughts.

Energy, picked up from others, is usually felt first within the body, which then alerts the mind. If the energy is uncomfortable it may cause emotional irritation. The mind and body will then work together, through thought and emotion, to rationalize this foreign energy invasion, which can activate prickly emotions. The prickly emotions then activate prickly thoughts that often become darker with the more attention given. This keeps us stuck in a repetitive cycle of uncomfortable thoughts and emotions.

Damaging Thoughts

One thing Empaths do too much of is thinking. Thoughts can take over our lives. It is a habit most need to get under control.

We cannot see or touch thoughts but we know they are there. Thoughts are energy; they create our reality and determine how we interpret the world.

Benign thoughts do no damage, but when they are dark, marauding or angry they will cause harm. If we often have thoughts in the shape of strong opinions, we may find they shape our life.

Thoughts create our reality and outlook, they can make us happy, angry or sad and are part of our belief system. Thoughts are behind our decisions; and lead us into trouble or out of danger. In life, our thoughts hold the reins. The last thing we want is an unbalanced mind caused by destructive thoughts.

We have on average 48 thoughts per minute or 50,000 to 70,000 thoughts a day... That's a lot of thinking.

Negative thoughts often take precedence in our mind. We can brood for hours on dark menacing thoughts whilst positive ones can be fleeting and go unnoticed. This is because humans are hardwired into having more negative thoughts than positive; it's a condition called negativity bias that stems back to our survival instincts from caveman days.

Thinking bad thoughts now and then isn't such a bad thing; it keeps life interesting. The problems happen when we get caught up in the negative thought process; it shapes our life into something we may not want.

Thoughts that are fleeting do no harm when they are second-long flickers. It is when they are repetitive, angry or resentful that they become damaging. To an aware Empath these thoughts feel dreadful and they will do anything to stop or control them.

'The only thing we control in our lifetime is our thoughts and actions... make them good!'

Thoughts and actions are the only thing humans are in complete control of. We have a choice of how we behave and think, but only when we become aware. Before we can regain control of our thoughts, we first we have to understand what takes that control away in the first place.

The Ego

When thoughts are uncontrolled the ego can do its worst work.

We all know how the ego operates: it is cunning and creates a 'them and us mentality', often making us feel like a victim.

The voice of the ego convinces us that everyone else is wrong and we are always right.

If the ego is allowed to be the voice within our head, we not only get taken away from our true path, and life purpose, but we get stuck in a place of no growth and movement.

The ego doesn't like to lose, fail, be judged or criticized, and to avoid disappointment or failure it will convince us not to take any leaps in life. It will keep us within our comfort zone and prevent us from making any waves or reaching our true potential. The ego likes to mask itself as fear.

It is the ego who kicks up the biggest fuss in the Empath's mind and is easily offended and wounded by others.

The ego likes to keep us stuck with outdated opinions and won't allow us to hear a voice suggesting change or one that contradicts its beliefs. It will always put up a fight.

If you are planning on making any changes to your life, the ego will protest loudly. Uncertainty and doubt is often triggered by the ego.

The more out-of-balance the Empath, the more the voice of the ego takes over and the unhappier one becomes.

I am, of course, giving you the worst case scenarios here but learning to recognize the voice of the ego, and working to still it, allows us to free ourselves from its grip and liberates us from an enslaved mind.

Here are some ways the ego likes to work:

- The ego convinces us we are better than others
- The ego wants to be the best at everything

- The ego gets overly hurt by criticism
- The ego likes to judge others
- The ego fears judgement
- The ego keeps us in fear of change
- The ego never feels complete and always wants more
- The ego worries about what others think
- The ego wants others to be envious
- The ego likes to be seen looking flashy
- The ego fears being classed as inferior
- The ego needs to be right
- The ego gets angry if anyone disagrees with its opinions
- The ego likes to hang out in victim-mentality
- The ego likes separation

The best way to calm our thoughts and quieten an over-zealous ego is through meditation and mind stilling exercises (see The Miracle of Meditation).

It is difficult to recognize the ego's power when the mind is noisy and this is why stilling our mind helps us define our true-self from the ego.

The ego can be likened to an internal prison, sneakily built, right under our noses. The input from others, expectations laid down by society and the fear of not fitting in, build higher prison walls.

We have the power to take the ego down, tame our unruly thoughts and bring our Empath mind into balance.

Before this can happen we first need to understand how the body and spirit can keep us from finding this balance...

4

The Living Vessel

The body is our physical vessel which houses the spirit and mind. Most Empaths are unaware just how out-of-balance their body is, or how this reflects in their sensitivity, emotional health and overall wellbeing.

Creating a strong, healthy body is essential if we want to find balance of the trinity and live a happy, healthy life.

When we first set out on our quest for self-improvement, the first place we normally start is by balancing the mind, through meditation, and increasing our spiritual awareness. But these practices will have little impact if we continue to consume anything that damages the body.

Empath Eating

We really are what we eat. It may seem tedious to be told the importance of improving the diet, but for the Empath it is an essential component to finding balance.

Many will only turn to changing their diet as a last resort, after trying everything else. Most do not want to know just how destructive the diet is to Empath health because food has such a powerful emotional hold.

Changing the diet may seem like one of the hardest things to do, especially giving up much loved foods, but it really isn't. Only our thoughts and addictions make the idea of eliminating certain foods a torturous idea.

We may hope we will be one of the few lucky ones, not affected by what we eat (a handful of people aren't), but being Sensitive means the majority of Empaths will have some changes they need to make.

Our body weakens with age and this means we have to put more effort into finding balance. What we could happily eat or drink in our twenties, can act as poison in our forties. Eating foods that weaken the body will take down the trinity.

It is widely believed that if there is no ill-effect shortly after eating a certain food it is safe to eat. This is not true. Adverse food reactions may not show up in the body or mind for up to forty-eight hours after consumption. And even then, the symptoms may seem minor.

Here is just a sample of what harmful food reactions look like: depression, fatigue, dry skin or skin irritations, weak fingernails and hair, itchy eyes, bloating, indigestion, back problems, mood swings, emotional sensitivities and weighted emotions, lack of drive and willpower, low confidence, excess introversion, weight issues and bowel problems. There are many, many more.

Drug-like, processed food, filled with chemicals, and foods we are intolerant to, not only deplete the body but affect our hormones and endocrine glands, lower our moods and, in some cases, cause severe mental disorders.

Just recently I watched a program about a young woman who suffered extreme mental disorders since her mid-teenage years. I will call her Clare.

Clare, who labelled herself as being "sensitive", had been a happy, kind and caring child. This all changed when she hit the teenage years. Almost overnight Clare started experiencing violent mood swings, sulky petulant behavior and deep depression. At first it was assumed this was just a teenage transition, causing the changes, but it soon became obvious it wasn't.

Over the years, her depression got so bad that Clare attempted suicide twice and had to be sectioned for her own safety. All the medical establishment could do was put her on powerful anti-psychotic drugs and anti-depressants to control her condition.

The medication allowed Clare to function within the world, to a certain degree, and stopped the suicidal tendencies, but did not change her moods or lift her depression.

Clare told the camera how she had lived in constant fear of plunging back into her dark depressive state, that led to her previous suicide attempts. She felt vulnerable, weak and not in control. The medication Clare took also caused unpleasant side-effects.

When she went to college, Clare decided to study holistic medicine in a bid to help her find a cure for her own problems. On enrollment she met the holistic teacher/practitioner who was taking the course. As soon as she laid eyes on Clare, the teacher informed her that she could see from her skin that she suffered with undiagnosed food allergies.

On her teacher's recommendation, Clare had a series of allergy and intolerance food tests done. The results showed her teacher to be correct, Clare was diagnosed with a dairy and soya intolerance.

When she removed all traces of soya and dairy from her diet, Clare's life gradually transformed. Her dark melancholy lifted and she was able to come off all her medication. She no longer had any depressive thoughts and, for the first time since she was a teenager, Clare felt really happy.

In case you think the transformation could have just been coincidental, Clare relayed a time when she unwittingly consumed a small amount of soya, in her salad dressing. Within hours of unknowingly ingesting the soya her mood plummeted and she was engulfed in an emotional darkness and deep despondency that lasted for days. This dreadful reaction came after Clare ingested only a small amount of soya.

The reason I share this story with you is to highlight the damage food can have on mental and physical health. These foods do not have to be classed as "unhealthy" for them to be destructive. If they are not compatible with your body chemistry, they can be damaging to your physical and mental health.

Most have no idea just how much the diet can affect the mind and body. I too have experienced incredible mood slumps after consuming certain foods and know only too well how it affects Empath traits. I have worked for some years on adapting my diet for better health and Empath wellbeing and I cannot tell you how utterly transformative it is from a perspective of being Sensitive.

I could not have imagined what an impact diet has on our emotional health or the way we pick up and process emotions belonging to others. There was a lot of trial and error with certain foods, but the cleaner my diet became the more I grasped the impact of our food and how it affects the mind, emotions, physical and energetic bodies.

If I eat poorly or choose foods that don't agree with me, it lowers my vibration. When my vibration lowers, my aura becomes more open and I pick up other peoples' energy easily. I also react to other people's energy differently.

It is essential that anyone who is Sensitive gets to grip with their diet. Whatever goes into your body, via the mouth, affects your mind. Poor food choices heighten all negative emotional responses and will cause unnecessary heartache. Here are just some of the reactions you can expect:

- Paranoia
- Increased emotional sensitivities
- Depression and low moods
- Mood swings
- Overreacting to other people's energy
- Irrational fears and phobias
- Excessive introversion

Our intuition is always at work, behind the scenes, trying to get our attention about how to care for ourself. But, too often, these promptings go unnoticed for the simple reason we are unaware of their importance.

In holistic-health circles it is known that it's easier to get an alcoholic to stop drinking than it is to get the average person to change their diet. Foods that don't agree with our genetic codes are often the ones we become addicted to and are destructive to our health.

Ask yourself now what food could you not live without?

The answer to that question will more than likely show you the food you are intolerant to or is damaging to your mental health. I expect it will be a food that either contains wheat, sugar, or some type of dairy as they are the foods known to cause the worst damage.

When it comes to your diet, take note of any physical ailments and emotional sensitivities. Now you are aware of how destructive your diet can be, food-related imbalances will be easier to spot

The quiet voice of your inner-guardian is always guiding you. When your intuition wants to make you aware of necessary change, the subject will keep popping into your mind. You may find yourself being drawn to certain websites, books or magazines, that contain information on nutritional health and wellbeing. For example: you may have had thoughts about eliminating refined sugar, and when you walk past a newsstand you notice all the magazines with articles relating to sugar elimination, you may go into a bookshop and the books that, jump out at you, all relate to sugar-free lifestyles or, when surfing the internet, you come across posts on the hazards of consuming refined sugar. These little pointers are your intuition's way of getting your attention and it is always sensible to listen.

Empaths are not only affected by the quality of their food, but the environment it was prepared in, who it was made by and whether or not it was created by nature or modified in a lab by man. Chemicals, lectins (plants natural defensive mechanism), negative energy, certain proteins and many other substances can create havoc within the imbalanced Empath.

Sensitive people have many levels of sensitive and this is why it is a challenge for some Empaths to pinpoint exactly where their imbalances lie, because there may be more than one.

Meat and Poultry

Some Empaths stop eating meat and poultry, even if they like the taste, because it does not feel right to them. The reason is often because they feel the energy of the animal's distress, in the form of residual energy. The vibration of an animal's suffering can bring the Empath's energy down. They may not be aware that this is how it affects them, simply because they have not made the connection.

But many Empaths become conscious of the energetic compatibility of their food the more aware they are.

The diet affects the mind, body and spirit. If the Empath eats food that has low-level energy, acts as an allergen or is drug-like it will impact their whole system and their traits.

It is important for all Empaths to come to understand how their food influences their ways. The best way to do this is by listening to what the body is telling you. If, for example, you suspect dairy is causing you allergic reactions, you could try the 30-day exclusion. This involves abstaining from all dairy, or whatever you suspect does not agree with you be it wheat, sugar, alcohol or meat, for 30 days. Then, after that time, gradually introduce it back into your diet. If you are intolerant, allergic or energetically incompatible you will have a big reaction on its reintroduction. If you suffer an ill-effect to a certain food, it is best removing it from your diet.

The Energy of Food

Empaths react to drug-like foods, more than those not of a sensitive nature, because they are highly reactive.

High reactive people taste the bitterness in lemons more than others, feel emotional and physical pain more intensely, go red in the face easier and are impacted by drugs and alcohol to a greater degree.

High reactives are acutely responsive to different vibrations of energy.

Everything is energy vibrating at different frequencies and that includes food, drugs or alcohol: the faster the vibration, the higher the frequency. Empaths are negatively affected by anything of a low vibration. Most processed, or drug-like foods, chemicals and alcohol have a low vibrational energy and will bring the Empath down fast.

Food prepared in an angry or unhappy environment carries that same energy and will show up within the Empath when consumed. The majority of Empaths will benefit from eating home-cooked food, so they know exactly what energy goes into their meals.

If the body is out of alignment, from the consumption of an unsuitable diet, chances are the mind and spirit will also be out of balance. It will make no difference if the body is toned and athletic, if it is being fed an allergen, anti-nutrient or drug-like food, or if the food has low emotional energy attached to it, the

Empath's balance will be thrown out of unison. The same applies when consuming any food which is artificial, genetically modified or hybridized.

Most already have an inkling of what they should or shouldn't consume, because our inner Knowing is always talking to us. Those nagging feelings, that something is not a fit, is the intuition, or higher-self, at work trying to get our attention. But, as humans, we have a weakness for the forbidden fruit and don't always want to listen to our guidance's recommendations.

Most Empaths are being poked, prodded and, in some cases, violently shook for them to pay attention and make changes to their diet and lifestyles.

Here are some of the ways you may be experiencing these inner prompts:

- If you use alcohol, to help get you through social situations, you find yourself getting intoxicated quickly and become so ill after consumption it feels like you could die.

  Hangovers last for days. Or you may keep having unfortunate drink-related accidents or incidents.

- After eating meat, poultry or fish you feel more depressed than normal and your energy levels plummet.

- You may find the kick start coffee in the morning giving you the jitters, making you anxious and/or nauseous.

- White sugar (or anything refined) makes your body instantly lethargic and your mind race.

- You feel fatigued, down and unhealthy. You have a weighted heaviness on your chest, like an inner-sadness, that won't go away.

- You are constantly unhappy, cannot find a light at the end of the tunnel, and are unable to get out of the slump.

When you take heed of your body's warning signals and remove whatever is lowering your vibration, you effectively release yourself from its control.

The wrong diet is draining and toxic to the Empath. If your body, mind or intuition is telling you it's time to give something up it would be prudent to listen. If you want to learn more about drug-like food and how it massively impacts the Empath's emotional and physical pain, please see my book 7 Secrets of the Sensitive.

Body Movement

Our bodies need to move regularly. Not to just to become slim or toned, but to keep stagnant energy moving away from us and keep our invisible body healthy.

A weak, inflexible, lethargic, unused and unworked body creates disruptions within the Empath mind, body and spirit. Certain exercises can be transformative for the Empath, as they can be for anyone, but most do not know or understand of their importance.

Movement is essential to an Empath's wellbeing. It works not only the physical but also the energetic body, and can help clear stagnant or negative energy.

Sadly, we live in a society that promotes a 'no-pain-no-gain' philosophy towards exercise and a focus on sculpting the muscles and reshaping the silhouette, rather than healing the body and mind.

There are so many ways to exercise and it doesn't have to be costly or complicated. It can be as simple as turning on some funky music and shaking your hips around the kitchen. Dancing when no one is watching is unbelievably uplifting and you get to make your own moves with the beat of the music.

Running, walking or cycling outdoors, freestyle dance, where there are no rules, or one of the many forms of yoga are some of the best forms of exercise for the Empath. These can be done alone and at home, and there is no need for a gym membership. Swimming in the sea or a lake (with no chemicals) is also a great way to move the body and clear low-level energy.

Comfort Zone

Allowing yourself to step out of your comfort zone, on a daily basis, allows for growth in all areas of your life. It enables you to face your fears which, in facing them, gives you a greater capacity to deal with negative emotions. When we stay comfortable, we stay small and don't expand. As the saying goes:

'If it doesn't challenge you it doesn't change you!' - Fred Devito

There are many ways to step from the comfort zone but an achievable way of doing it is by going further than you would like during exercise. Staying within the confines of what feels comfortable, during exercise, keeps you within the same mental and physical place. Going beyond, gives you a sense of achievement and a gritty determination towards all that you would like to achieve in life.

 'As one goes through life one learns if you don't paddle your own canoe, you don't move'. Katherine Hepburn

Lack of exercise, an unsuitable diet and consumption of stimulants or drug-like substances prevents you from finding Empath balance, fact!

An out-of-balance body compromises our thoughts and emotions, disrupts our hormones and endocrine glands, which then impedes the function of the chakras, and leaves our energy-field wide open. If you change your diet and you will change your life!

5

Magic of the Spirit

The spirit is the invisible us. Our spirit is the most important part of Self and comprises of our soul (spirit or eternal self), the energy centers (chakras) and the aura (also known as the energy sheath, energy-field, energetic, electromagnetic body and more).

What plays the biggest part in keeping the Empath from finding balance is a diminished or damaged energy-field.

Your aura emanates around you like a luminous egg-shaped sheath. It extends around and away from the body for anything up to five feet (in a healthy person). The vibration of this energetic body is fine and subtle.

Those who are unhealthy, in their body and mind, have an unhealthy, receded aura which is also permeable (energy leaks out and in).

The aura has seven layers to it corresponding with the seven main chakras. Working to balance the chakras results in a more balanced aura.

Our aura both surrounds and penetrates our body and resonates with both our physical and mental bodies. Years' worth of data is stored within our energy-field; this information is normally an accumulation of happy and sad life experiences, ideas and opinions, unreleased painful emotions, negative thought-forms, past life memories and toxins, etc. Because Empaths pick up energy from others, we can also carry within our aura their negative thought-forms and energy.

A weakened body and mind weakens our energetic body (aura). Low-level thoughts and emotions, unbalanced chakras, food intolerances, poor diet, drugs and alcohol all impair the body, and anything that debilitates the body damages our aura.

When the aura is damaged it becomes leaky. This is bad news on many levels: it allows our energy out (causing fatigue and other imbalances), and allows other people's energy in which then merges with our own.

Empaths are known to have a permeable aura and this is why people's energy can be so debilitating. But they are not the only ones. Anyone who is unhealthy or with emotional issues possess a weakened energy-field, which means their energy and emotions are also able to leak out.

If an Empath comes into close proximity with those who have a leaky aura they will soak up any leaked energy like a super-absorbent sponge. It may appear that strangers' energy purposely infringes our own, but it is often an energetic merger.

If you are unhealthy, eat an unsuitable diet, take drugs or stimulants, drink alcohol, smoke cigarettes, experience stress and have dark thoughts you will likely have a permeable aura. This means you will pick the emotions and energy off others easily and they will become etched within your energy-field. You will also be affected by negative residual energy and other low frequency energy. The only way to heal the aura is by making changes.

Experiencing overwhelm, after picking up other people's energy, means the memory of it will often become imprinted. Any future interactions, with unfamiliar energy, may cause something like an "energetic allergic reaction". These reactions are draining and can leave us feeling well below par for hours or even days. If these responses become a common occurrence, following time spent in public places, it will prevent us from fully participating in our own life. This can be seen by avoidance of peopled areas and anything that involves social interaction.

By finding total balance of mind, body and spirit, it works something like an "energetic anti-histamine" for the Empath. A healthy body and mind results in a powerful aura and creates the Empath's invisible armour. A powerful aura empowers the Empath. It persuades other people's energy to bounce off and is key to living a happier life.

We cannot expect our mind and spirit to be strong when we are putting something into the body that weakens it. Nor can we expect our body to be strong if we experience "Sensitivity stress".

Sensitivity Stress

Empaths are Sensitive. Anyone who is Sensitive will experience powerful emotions, vivid thoughts and imagination, and they will get hurt easily. This can lead to Sensitivity stress which compromises the immune system and health, and results in a damaged aura.

Sensitivity stress is endured by those who experience emotions powerfully, get upset easily or experience other people's energy as an adverse reaction (feeling drained, experiencing negative emotion or becoming unwell), they also overreact to any emotional situation and are prone to having anxiety or panic attacks.

This type of stress is not caused by having deadlines to work to and a mammoth to-do-list (although they certainly won't help), it is caused by having a Sensitive nature, being overly stimulated from external energy and/or having buried emotional pain. Just like normal stress, it damages the immune system and puts strain on the mind and body. This in turn leads to illness, rampant thoughts and a weakened aura.

Finding Balance

Finding balance of the mind, body and spirit takes time for the simple reason we don't always know where an imbalance lies. But, generally, when we heal the mind and body the energetic body can often take care of itself, unless there is powerful emotional debris stored within it.

Sometimes the aura can have become damaged nearly beyond repair. This generally happens when one has suffered an incredibly traumatic experience caused by any of the following: enduring difficulties as an infant, during childbirth or whilst in the womb, severe sickness in childhood, an unexpected bereavement or traumatic loss, or any type of trauma that acted as a catalyst for a huge emotional shift. If you know your body is strong and healthy (after making changes), but have a weakened aura (by suffering a traumatic life experience), then you are still at risk of picking up the emotional energy off others. There are ways to protect yourself from taking on foreign energy (see Protective Shielding) which will also help build a stronger energy body.

As already mentioned, the best way to heal the aura is by balancing the body and mind but if you want to speed the process up, a visit to a holistic or spiritual healer will help put you on the path to healing your energy-field.

Holistic and Spiritual Healing

Many Empaths are born healers, or are at least open to the concept, and will find most holistic treatments beneficial (we just need to remember we also have to make the inner-changes and not to rely solely on a healer).

A healer can come in the form of a reflexologist, massage therapist, Indian head massage technician, homeopath, shaman, color therapist and more. Anyone who works on your body, holistically, also works on the energy-field, if even inadvertently. Some of the best therapies to heal the energy-field are those which work with the subtle energies of the chakras, meridians and the aura. Treatments such as reiki, crystal therapy, chakra alignments, spiritual and shamanic healing are perfect for strengthening and balancing the aura.

If you are one who finds it difficult to relax, combining a physical-treatment such as reflexology, Thai massage or any other type of massage, with an energy-balancing treatment will go a long way towards alignment of the trinity.

Healers are also known to lend a caring ear. And, with your permission, they will often guide you towards finding any buried emotional pain and help release it.

Finding a healer, who is also a match, is often where the challenge lies. An Empath needs to be able to completely trust those they choose to share their pain with and they need to feel energetically compatible.

Although those who choose healing as a profession tend to be trustworthy and are there to assist, not all of them will be a match for the Empath. A bad match is often felt as a clash of energy. When there is a clash, one feels uncomfortable or unable to open up with the chosen healer. This does not denote the healer is incapable, but there will be a contradiction in emotional compatibility. It is often worth having a consultation with a therapist/healer to see if they feel right before booking a treatment.

Finding a healing therapist should not require much more than a good internet search. Allowing your intuition to guide you towards the correct healer is helpful (see next chapter), as is getting recommendations from your friends on social media, or those who live local to you.

Remember you will not receive the full benefits of any treatment if your body is out-of-balance, or if you are refusing to give up destructive behaviors. But everything happens in small steps. You cannot expect a transformation to happen overnight, nor would you want it to.

The changes we make and the experiences we have, both the good and bad, are all part and parcel of this amazing, mystical journey. Be patient with yourself. Rome was not built in a day. Just know that every step you take is a step in the right direction.

Spiritual Awakenings

It is common, as an Empath, to have a sudden spiritual awakening. These appear in many ways and each of us can experience them differently. I thought it worth mentioning here because spiritual awakenings can sometimes be scary when one does not understand what is happening.

When enduring a spiritual awakening, you may believe that you are going slightly cuckoo, with the experiences it involves. You may also feel alone and not know where to turn.

If now wondering what the difference is between an Empath and spiritual awakening: the former is where one's inherent Empathic attributes kick in and heighten, the latter is where the experiences tend to be more spiritual or psychic in nature.

A spiritual awakening can happen in many ways: you may start to experience elaborate visions foretelling future events, hear waves of hushed voices, in your head, as if someone is trying to communicate, you may sense intense energy around you, feel a pulsating sensations in your third eye (center of forehead), suddenly know information about people that you shouldn't and other psychic phenomenon, you may be subjected to sudden electrical charges within the body or find yourself often being zapped by static. There are many other signs but these are some of the the most common.

An awakening can make you feel lost at first, but it is normally just the sign of transitioning times. If you suspect you are having one, you will want as much information as you can get on the subject. By typing the words 'spiritual awakening' into any internet search engine a wealth of information will come up to feast your eyes upon.

The more unusual aspects, of an awakening, will normally subside of their own accord, but if you feel you need help, or one-on-one advice, a good place to start is by visiting a spiritual circle, healer, shaman, or one who knows a lot about spiritual energy.

Like the Empath awakening, a spiritual one is just a way to put you on a new path. It simply means you are ready for the next level and your awareness has opened up to take you there. It may also be a sign, from your higher self, to push you towards building your intuition.

6

Empath Intuition

Having strong intuition, we can trust, becomes an advantage when navigating the turbulent journey of Empath life.

Luckily, Empaths are born with a powerful sense of awareness which we can continue to build over the course of our lives.

Tuning into our intuition, and developing it, will save us a lot of unnecessary setbacks when it comes to making life-decisions. It will guide us towards the right path, prevent us from making poor choices and keeps us from those who would do us harm.

Our intuition also helps explain life's complexities and gives us greater understanding of why we are here and what our purpose is.

Each of us is important and unique, and the paths we walk are individual to us.

In the early stages of discovering our birthright we may need marked signs, laid out for us by another, to point us is the right direction. But in the grander scheme, the best person to tell you what path to take is you.

Developing your intuition will give you the ability to trust your quiet guiding voice, and inner-promptings, and, in doing so it will serve you forever!

Being able to hear your intuition, and trust its insights, will guide you to the life you are meant to lead. The best way to do this is by learning its many signals, which are often unique to each of us. For example: when faced with a certain decision, we may get an uncomfortable nagging feeling in the solar-plexus region (gut-area). This is our intuition informing us that it is not a good choice. We may ignore this feeling, or our ego may shout over it, but they happen for a reason.

The "feelings" within our solar-plexus region are coming from what is known as our second brain, the gut. The sensations come from the enteric nervous system, a network of neurons lining our gut and responsible for the "butterflies", felt in the stomach.

Our emotions are influenced by our gut nerves. The saying 'trust you gut' should always be heeded by the Empath. We ought to listen and trust our gut sensations as it is one of the fastest ways to experience our basic intuitive instinct.

Everyone experiences excitement, fear, nervousness and insightful inklings in the gut area, but as Sensitives we feel these impressions with gusto.

When we recognize what the different sensations represent, our inner Knowing will guide us through life simply by the way something feels. The more attuned we become, the better we are at differentiating between these predictive gut responses.

When it comes to decision-making, and using the intuition as a guide, always note how everything feels. If a certain choice causes feelings of distress or dread (that aren't stemming from a fear of change), then that choice is not a good one. If the decision feels calm, peaceful or uplifting then that choice is safe.

Ask the questions you want to know the answers to then gauge how it feels. This approach can be used before taking any action.

By developing your intuition, you will learn to understand the sensations you experience and what they represent. You can then distinguish between what is an irrational fear and an inner-warning, and know how to discern between the right path and the easy path (the easy path often turns out to be the hardest).

As an Empath, you may be swayed by other people's ideas, opinions or thoughts but always stop and listen to your own awareness, it has more power than you know.

Your true-self will guide you in the direction you are meant to go and it will give you the answers you need to keep on track.

It is worth bearing in mind that we don't always get the answers we want to hear. This is the biggest cause of people ignoring their intuitive guidance.

If our guidance goes against what we have mentally mapped out, or our heart's desire, we don't always want to hear its urgings.

Another issue the Empath has to recognise is whether the ego has a strong influence over the mind. When this is the case we may be more inclined to listen to its all-pervasive voice than to our deep inner-promptings.

The ego follows the "materialistic herd". It wants the things that do not always serve one's growth. The ego wants to appear grandeur and to look better and be better in every way.

The ego takes great offence if anyone should disagree with its opinions and will push to follow a life based on what an elitist society dictates, as opposed to what the soul needs for nourishment and growth.

Much unhappiness in the world is caused by people listening to their ego instead of their soul.

Banishing the persuasive voice of ego is part of developing as an Empath, and a human, in doing so it allows us to realign with our intuitive higher-self which then becomes our guiding-force.

Luckily, most Empaths are highly aware of the ego and try not to allow it to run the show. When our intuition develops, it zones in on any sneaky interferences, from ego, before it can influence our decisions.

Building intuition is simple, but requires effort. There are some straightforward steps that, when followed, will put you on a fast-tracked-path to opening your awareness.

Here is a quick reference to get you started:

1. Practice meditation daily. If only for a short time, five minutes a day is better than no minutes.

Stilling the mind through meditation is the best way to develop intuition. It is not an overnight process and some have to work harder to quieten the mind than others. (See next chapter.)

It is in meditation you receive the answers to your questions through messages and visions.

2. Know your visions are real. The visions you see in meditation are real and have significant meaning… we just need to decipher them.

Many of our messages come through symbolism or code and are unique to each one of us. Learning to decode them is essential to understanding them. For example: one person may see a red rose in their mind's eye and interpret it as message of love; another may see the same, but interpret the thorns and color red as a sign of danger.

Our visions and messages are exclusive to us and that is why it is important to recognize their meanings and believe in them.

3. Keep a meditation diary. After each meditation, quickly write down what you saw and felt, even if it wasn't much. This goes a long way to helping you decipher your visions.

If you don't write what you saw you will soon forget.

You often get messages during meditation that may make no sense for days, weeks or even months after you received them. One day you will come to understand what your message was trying to tell you through the notes you made.

A meditation diary will also help you interpret and understand any repetitive imagery.

4. Listen to your feelings. Your solar-plexus is your seat of emotions. It is here we get to experience our intuitive feelings.

For decision making, always tune into the solar-plexus intuition. If a certain choice causes feelings of distress or discomfort, then that choice is a poor one. If, however, the decision feels calm, peaceful or uplifting, then that choice is safe for us.

5. Take intuition development or meditation classes. A supportive group environment is a perfect place to increase intuition and sixth-sense.

The power of the like-minded working collectively, in meditation, can enhance intuitive awareness.

Always listen to your inner-vibes when choosing a class. It has to feel completely safe and hopefully be an ego-free zone.

6. Note the intuitive events you experience each day. This can be done in your meditation diary.

Intuitive events happen every day. When you think of a person and they suddenly call or you follow a hunch that proves to be accurate, these are messages from your intuition. There are many more.

However small or insignificant they seem, your intuition is at work guiding you. Too often these happenings are brushed off as coincidence. Writing them down is confirmation of how your sixth-sense is increasing. The more you develop, the more you will notice these goings-on.

7. Stay in balance, mentally and physically. Eating right and looking after the body through exercise helps intuition develop.

An unhealthy out-of-balance body is a very poor conductor of psychic energy.

When you have a sluggish body you will have slow-moving energy centers and a foggy mind. Visions will have no clarity or focus, and the inclination to progress will be stalled (see my book 7 Secrets of the Sensitive).

Follow Your Heart

Some may sense intuitive sensations around their heart area, but this tends to happen when one has spent time working on self and spirituality.

When the heart opens we know we are on the right path: Our sense of gratitude and wonder of life knows no bounds, we gain deeper insight into the purpose of everything and the difference between right and wrong choices becomes unmistakable.

An open heart is a goal worth working towards. The heart opens when we attain balance, build our intuition and aim to be the best version of ourselves.

With the opening of the heart, magic happens and a world of wonder is revealed. Again, this is not an overnight process, but knowing it is achievable for everyone should be enough to keep us striving towards it.

It is mostly, but not always, during meditation, when we first become aware of the powerful heart opening. It is difficult to describe, but once you experience it you know exactly what it is. After your first taste, you will want to feel the opened heart all the time.

Everything that weakens the Empath: mind, body and spirit, will also prevent the heart opening.

If you are one who has experienced the heart's opening intermittently, this is completely normal, especially in the beginning stages. However, if you felt it once, some time ago, but never again, you are doing something in your life which is preventing your heart from opening further. This is where your intuition can once again serve you.

By tuning in, during meditation, you can find answers to many of life's questions, such as what is impeding your intuitive awareness or heart opening.

Before you sit down to meditate ask questions such as: 'What is preventing my intuition developing?' or 'What is blocking my heart opening?' Then, whilst in meditation listen for your answers. Simple!

To receive reliable guidance, during your meditation, you need to have a committed daily routine. By developing your practice, it will serve in many more amazing ways than just developing your inner guidance. Let's take a look...

7

The Miracle of Meditation

Not only is meditation a pathway to emotional freedom for the Empath, and a journey into the unknown, it is also an essential part of balancing the trinity of mind, body and spirit. I know I keep repeating the importance of balancing the trinity, throughout the book, but it is super important.

It doesn't matter what you do for self-development and improvement, if the trinity are not equally stabilized you will struggle with your Empath abilities.

Being able to unplug from the energy of others and set energetic boundaries, requires a quiet mind.

When our mind is noisy, stressed or distracted we let our "energetic" guard down. This means we easily open up to other people's stuff, which is not so easy to switch off.

Through meditation, the mind becomes strong. A strong mind helps us to set the necessary boundaries required to protect from the energy of others. It allows us to unplug from the energetic connections to people, that make Empath life challenging, it also builds intuition.

For an Empath, learning to control the mind is also a prerequisite to a happy, healthy life. It is after all our thoughts that create our outlook on reality. Our thoughts and feelings are interconnected: the way we think about anything reflects in how we feel about it.

Our thoughts are catalyst to building feelings of anger, fear and sadness, etc. Yet, what some don't realize, we have a choice over our thoughts. They do not need to control us and make life a misery.

A busy mind has one thought after another flowing through. It is said the average person has at least 35 thoughts a minute. Our thoughts keep us up at night and wake us in the morning. They take over our mind when we are driving (how often have you got somewhere without remembering the journey?) and stop us from noticing what is going on around us. In other words, they distract us from life.

Being able to quieten the mind through meditation takes time and effort. But in doing so, you allow time for you. By practicing meditation, it does not mean you will never have thoughts again; you will simply be able to control the unnecessary ones.

Empaths absorb other people's emotions into their energy-field like a sponge. Once a thought becomes attached to emotions, picked up off another's emotional pain, you claim full ownership of them. Emotions and thoughts work hand in hand. An emotion activates a thought and the thought stimulates the emotion, which then activates a physical sensation.

When we gain mastery over our mind we have a greater ability to switch off the thoughts activated by another person's energy.

Many people get put off the idea of meditation because they think it involves crouching on the floor, in a limb-twisting lotus position, whilst wearing a turban and giant nappy. This is not how meditation looks... Although perfectly acceptable for those who wish. Meditation is simply a way to still the mind and it can be done whilst sitting in your favorite chair, in the office, sat in the park, or even on the toilet.

Meditation is not difficult but then it also isn't easy. As long as you devote a certain length of time each day to the practice you will see amazing changes to your Empath life. Start with five minutes and build up. If your life is super busy, and you don't have five minutes to spare, practice for three. The only thing that stops us meditating is excuses.

There are many ways to meditate and they don't all involve sitting down quietly with the eyes closed. Here are just some ways: mindfulness, chanting, breath-work, visualization, trance, and yoga. Yes, yoga is considered a moving meditation, and is a good option for those who do not like to sit still.

You don't have to stay in-doors either. You can do a walking meditation. This is performed by externalizing your awareness and focus on everything around you as you observantly stroll: Notice your feet on the pavement, or grass, as you walk or observe the greenery of the trees and cloud formations in the sky. If a random thought tries to distract you simply breathe through it and let it go.

Don't fight your thoughts during meditation. By fighting them it will cause an inner-conflict and greater distraction.

Our ego will always put up a fight to stay in control of the mind. It will find many ways to keep you distracted. For example: when you first start to meditate, you will find that the world and his wife have taken up residence in your head, all fighting to say their bit. This is entirely normal. Albeit somewhat frustrating. We should look at it as turbulence on a plane: when you push through you will climb above it and then all will become calm, smooth and serene.

Anything good in life does not happen overnight. Great things take time to develop. The problem many Empaths have is they often first turn to meditation when they are in a dark mental space.

When having any kind of life crisis our thoughts are at their darkest and most dominant. This makes quietening them a mammoth task. Many will give up on meditation before they have had chance to experience its real benefits.

In an ideal world, we would take preventative measures and start our meditation practice before we hit our "dark night of the soul," but as this is rarely the case, we need to find the best ways to settle into a meditation practice before throwing in the towel.

To begin a meditation practice, plan a set time every day. Morning is best when the day has not had chance to build in the mind. Perhaps start with five minutes. Having no distractions is important. If you think someone will walk in and disturb you that's all you'll think about. If there is a lot of external noise, pop some earphones in and play some gentle music, or listen to a guided meditation.

If you are one who finds it difficult to meditate, try it after performing some kind of vigorous exercise. Our mind is always at its calmest after strenuous physical activity and the pathway towards a quiet mind is more accessible.

Getting Out of Your Head

Negative thoughts are destructive to our health and wellbeing, especially when they are repetitive. Empaths occupy a lot of time in their heads. If they spend too much time around those who have a darkened energy signature, it will seep into the awareness, via the energy-field, and then into their mind. Igniting painful emotions, anger and thoughts of being wronged or unfairly treated (that often have nothing to do with said person).

You may not realize these irrational thoughts, that are on a perpetual loop, have been stirred by being around certain others, because they don't always kick-in till a while after exposure. Residual energy, taken from another, can hover in your energy-field for days or weeks. The weaker your energy-field the worse the effects. Learning to get out of your head (thoughts) also offers protection against the residual energy of others.

Change Your Thoughts

Many of us help create our life situations with the thoughts we keep, especially dark, repetitive ones. From the second a negative thought pops into our head we only have a matter of moments before its settles in and changes our mindset from positive to negative. Once this happens, one bad thought after another keeps rolling in. The best way to avoid it is not to indulge in the thought in the first place.

When a dark thought arises, change it immediately to a good one. Sounds simple, but often the simplest steps prove to be the most challenging.

We have a choice about what we think (and feel). We can allow our thoughts to rule us or we can rule our thoughts... Change your thoughts change your life!

The meditation below, is designed to quieten your mind but at the same time help build a stronger energy-field. It can be practiced daily.

Trinity Meditation

- Sit in a comfortable position with your back straight and close your eyes. Breathing through your nose, focus on your breath. Inhale for 3 seconds and exhale for 3 seconds. On the inhale feel your tummy expand and on the exhale feel it deflate, repeat a few times until you feel your focus go within.

- Next take your awareness to your third eye (center of forehead) and, in your mind's eye, see it in total darkness like a dark movie screen. Keep your focus on this dark, silky screen for several seconds.

- Now, whilst focusing on the screen, see a spec of golden light appear within its center, watch as it expands, transforming into a golden-sand footpath, winding off into the distance. The path is surrounded by lush fields filled with beautiful wild flowers and long gilded grass, gently swaying on a warm summer breeze. The sun is shining and it's a lovely day.

- See yourself following this path. Put yourself in the picture. Look at what you're wearing. Are you barefoot? Glance around, what can you see, hear and smell?

- Take your awareness back to the path and follow it until you come to a small, wooden bridge, crossing a shallow stream. Stop and observe the clear sapphire waters glimmering, like beautiful crystals, under the sunlight. The water flows swiftly but gently over onyx pebbles and gem-like tumble-stones. You can spend as much time as you like here, perhaps dip your toes into the stream or wade into the shallows, allowing the cool water to gently massage your calves and ankles.

- When you're ready, cross the bridge over to a huge old Oak tree on the other side. Observe the tree in all its glory: The gnarled and knotted bark of the trunk, leading up to the towering twisted branches above. See the beautiful lush green leaves radiating an intoxicating emerald aura that encompasses the entire tree. This the color of your heart center, it is both healing and balancing.

- Allow the aura of the tree to connect and merge with your own. This magnificent energy clears your entire aura of any negative emotion, painful past memories, or energy which does not belong.

- Now place your hands on the trunk of the Oak tree. Feel the incredible power surge through your hands, up your body and down into your feet. See energetic roots coming from the soles of your feet connecting you to the Earth and empowering you with healing energy.

- Take your hands away from the giant Oak but keep focusing on its power cursing through you. See this powerful energy expanding out into your energy-field. This energy heals and seals any porous parts of your aura and builds a shield of powerful protection. Keeping your energy in and others' energy out.

- Know this empowered energy-field is your protection and will keep you safe from harm. Stay here in this relaxed state for as long as you wish.

- When ready, open your eyes and take some refreshing breaths before getting on with your day.

8

The Impact of Residual Energy

Residual energy is a term all Empaths become familiar with. It is often used when describing the energy remnants left in objects, places or buildings by those who have gone before.

When a traumatic event has happened in an area it leaves a powerful imprint, within the energy, which Empaths, and anyone who is Sensitive, can pick up on. The same can be said if there has been a lot of anger, hate or erratic emotions within a particular place.

Certain rooms in most houses will contain a host of different vibes and residual energy. Bedrooms, where confused, angry or moody teens grew up, can acquire a dense energy stain. Living-rooms, where families relax and come together, often have a laid-back vibe.

I have always sensed residual energy within buildings and locations, but I did not always know what it was I sensed. When I was younger, if I felt a heavy energetic imprint in the places I visited, I believed the space was haunted. In some cases, the residual energy almost felt like a presence.

I used to naively believe dark residual energy within a house was a sign of malevolence. It took a while for me to understand it is mostly painful emotions and experiences that caused the dense energy and not some evil act (although that certainly leaves a dark mark).

Most buildings will contain some kind of residual energy. Empaths pick up on these vibes rather like first impressions. We notice them at first, but don't always continue to if we visit a place frequently.

Just like buildings that hold low-level residual energy, there are many places with happy vibes. When a house had been filled with a lot of love or happiness the building feels like the sun is shining indoors.

I remember a particular neighbors' house, from childhood, that had the sunshine energy. Mr and Mrs Motler were probably in their seventies when I knew them. They were the loveliest, kindest couple you could imagine to meet. They had a smile for everyone and were liked by all. Their loving energy could be felt in their home as warmth and safety. Long after they had passed away, and new neighbors moved in, the house still kept the powerfully positive imprint the Motlers left behind.

Energetic imprints can last for many years after they have formed and greatly affect the ambience of a place.

Empaths are affected by residual energy in many different ways. You may go to a place, or inside a building, and feel happy, sad, angry or depressed. It can even affect you physically, making you feel nauseated or faint. Depending on your Sensitivity, and the level of an energetic imprint, will depend on what you sense and how you react.

If a building is classed as "haunted" an Empath will feel the energy of a presence on entering, but it may be difficult to define from residual energy.

The energy of a spirit is often recognized when you feel a presence, or denser energy, at the same time as a dramatic temperature drop. The more aware you become the easier it is to identify between residual energy and spiritual energy.

I have been to places where there is both powerfully positive and darker energy within the same building.

Not so long ago, my husband and I came across a medieval church in fascinating little place in the Cotswolds, called Cirencester.

St Johns the Baptiste sat in the center of the bustling old town and immediately grabbed your attention by its very presence.

As the church was open to visitors, we decided to take a look around. When I first entered the church vestibule, the energy I picked up was similar to what other old churches feel like. But as I wandered through to the center aisles, I was hit by the most powerful energy. It felt incredible! Almost magical. It was so intoxicating it brought tears to my eyes. I wanted to hang out in it all day. I could not imagine what had created such an enchanting atmosphere.

As I made my way around the church, it became evident the same vibrant energy did not run through the entire building. Some parts had the usual "churchy" vibe, some felt darker and cold and others felt pleasant, but nothing in comparison to what I felt in the center of the church. Unfortunately, as we were watching the clock, I did not have time to stay and ponder the magnificent energy. But it is a place I intend to return to in the future and spend more time.

Although a lot of happy events and powerful prayers happen within most churches, there is also a lot of pain expressed within the walls. There are many who turn to the church when they are in deep crisis.

Most of the churches I have visited have had a similar vibe and I wouldn't really say it's always pleasant. Some have a distinct air of reverence and others a deep sense of sadness, but one of the main vibes I pick up on is fear and judgement.

When people have visited churches through the ages they are always on their best behavior, children and adults alike. Whatever is going on in their lives gets put on hold and the face they wear is not a true reflection of what is happening in their life. Hundreds of people carrying the worry of being judged or berated, for behaving out of turn, creates a powerful vibration and leaves a strong, dark energetic stain in a place, no matter how many other positive events happen within the same walls. This was why I was so surprised by the amazing energy of the church in Cirencester. One might say this energy was due to the power of prayer.

Prayers have incredibly powerful energy, but a prayer coming from love has a completely different vibration from one coming from fear or lack. Which, sadly, many prayers come from.

I'm sure many other places around the world carry the same amazing energy of St Johns. Locations where many people come together and express any kind of emotion creates a shift in the frequency; the stronger the emotions the deeper the imprint.

As an Empath, the effect of residual energy can greatly influence your balance. When it is positive and filled with warm vibrations it is empowering. Low-level energy can change your way of thinking, lower your moods and alter behavior and decisions. You will be aware that something is not right, when affected by this energy, although you may not be aware of its origin.

Energetic imprints influence everyone, not just the Sensitive. We've all heard of places where history repeats and bad things continue to reoccur: wars, accidents, arguments, etc. This is when unaware people pick up the low-level residual energy, take it on and re-enact the script. Low-level energy is contagious and can become destructive to the unaware or out-of-balance.

High mood residual energy is also contagious and vigorously uplifting. But because much of the populace are already in a downcast place, they tend to veer more easily towards the dark.

As humans, we are never happy when in a low mood but, ironically, most stay longer, by choice, in a dark mental space than in a positive one.

Sadly, much of our world has been manipulated to keep us down. When we go under emotionally, it proves to be a mammoth task to climb back up and out. This is why it is beneficial for all Empaths to learn to recognize negative, residual energy and work to stop it affecting them. We have the ability to project our mood. The last thing any of us would want to be responsible for, is taking down another as a result of taking on energy that did not belong to us.

Residual energy, from others, can seep into our aura and influence our thoughts and moods for days after being picked up.

Anyone and everyone can leave a dark mark of lingering energy when in a low mood, but those who affect Empaths in the most painful ways are the people who act as emotional trauma triggers (ETTs).

To those who are Sensitive, the mere mention of an ETT's name is enough to ignite an unpleasant emotional response. But the worst reaction happens when one has spent time in their presence and their imprint has infused into one's energetic body.

Trauma trigger people (who are often family members, friends or work colleagues, etc.) feel like poison to the Empath. Their presence can make us physically ill. And when their residual energy is undesirable, it can throw our body and mind into disarray for days or weeks.

When spending time with those who "press your buttons" it is easy to act in a defensive way, or out of character. Because you feel uncomfortable when with an ETT, it affects your attitude towards them.

If your mood lowers so will your vibration, this opens you up to picking up more of their residual energy.

You can protect yourself to a certain extent, from ETTs, by staying in a positive mind-set and not retaliating towards any unfair comments they make. By keeping your intention high, and speaking positive, power-filled words, it is empowering and uplifting. It also works in being protective. However, possessing an upbeat demeanor does not always shield you from a residual energy attack.

You normally experience an ETTs residual energy anything from a couple of hours up to a day or two after being in their presence. It feels like a psychic attack: you may find you cannot focus and get constantly distracted from everyday tasks, your mind keeps dipping into their conversations, and the intentions behind them, and you find yourself getting riled by their words' true meaning; even though you were not affected by them when they were said. You may experience anger, resentment and emotional discomfort; caused by dark residual energy.

These responses happen because you are still energetically connected to your trauma trigger. When you drop your guard you feel the impact.

Why Does This Happen?

As already discussed, the Empath's aura is often permeable which means they are energetically open and susceptible to picking up other people's "stuff". It also puts them at a disadvantage when spending time with those who act as trauma triggers.

When one's energy-field is leaky or open, residual energy, from people or places, seeps in and mixes with our own. If not cleared, this energy can linger for a long time and cause disruption.

Our aura is connected to our physical body. Anything negative picked up within the energy-field will disturb our body and mind, controlling our moods and thoughts.

If you know you get taken down by residual energy, after spending time with a certain person, it may be wise to avoid them. If this is not possible, only spend time with them when there is a group of people around. Always be pleasant and stay in your positive mental-space, but try not to get engaged in deep conversation. This will help keep you protected.

The sad part of this story is those who become trauma triggers to the Empath are often those who have the deepest hidden pain and insecurities, which they refuse to face. This pain is often shaped into selfish or conceited behavior, which then builds a dark cloud of residual energy. Regrettably, until they are willing to see their insecurities for themselves no one else can help them.

There is now a greater chance of you being affected by dark residual energy on regular occasions. We are in a time of great change. The world is shifting and people are in crisis! This crisis has no sight of ending anytime soon.

People are having many unresolved issues, emotional pain and insecurities coming up to the surface (AKA the shadow-side), because they need to be cleared. Many are trying to avoid facing their pain, which just makes it more disruptive. This then creates a lot of unpleasant residual energy which is picked up by the Empaths.

Here is a quick technique to protect against residual energy.

It only takes a couple of minutes to do and can be practiced before, or after, venturing into dense-energy places or when spending time around trauma triggers:

- Close your eyes, take some deep breaths and allow your body to relax.

- Take your attention to your heart center and see a beautiful light pulsating from it. See this light radiating out, encompassing your whole body, inside and out. See it expanding to at least 3 foot from the body, into a luminous oval sheath.

- Choose a color that makes you feel safe, warm and empowered and allow it to infuse your aura and encase the entire exterior.

- This is your powerful shield of protection. Acknowledge to yourself that you are now protected and you do not give permission for any uninvited energy to enter your sacred space.

9

Shielding

Living in this heavily populated world, Empaths are faced with many energetic challenges. If it is not being knocked out-of-balance, by picking up residual energy, they are sapped of their vitality by spending time around energy-drainers. Merely walking through public places can be enough to leave them weak and disheveled, and spending time in the presence of a certain family member can be the reason behind a week's worth of energy and emotional clearing.

Learning to set energetic boundaries is a given for those of a Sensitive nature. Many Empaths become hardwired into doing this, once they become aware of their birthright, but the newly awakened Empath often needs guidance. But sometimes, even the aware need gentle reminders of what they can do to protect themselves when out in public.

For the Empath, blocking out all external emotions and energies is often their first priority when on their path to awakening, but it is not always that cut-and-dry. She might have tried every energy-blocking technique known to man, without any success, and spent many hours in meditation, working to still the mind and rebalance the energy-field. But still the energy of others affects her.

No matter how in balance an Empath, they will always feel the emotions and energy of others, but they do not have to be taken down by them.

Striving for stability should become the Empath's priority in life. If we are destructively impacted, mentally and physically, by the world's inhabitants this is what we project onto others. Part of our role, as an Empath, involves helping to uplift the energy of others, which is difficult to do when we reside in a low-vibrational space.

Why Do Empaths Feel All They Do?

There is a question that always springs to mind at some point during the Empath's awakening: 'Why do

Empaths feel and take on what they do, emotionally, is it not for a purpose? In taking on these negative energies are they not helping rid the world of them?' These questions are debatable and it may well be there is no right answer, or it can only be answered by opinions.

Some will argue that the Empaths are here to help others (which I agree with) and need to get out into the world to help take away the emotional pain of others (which I don't completely agree with).

Yes, there are Empaths who assist in healing others. Yes, there are Empaths who help transmute negative energies. And yes, some Empaths will take away another's woes just by listening to them. BUT, if they themselves are very out-of-balance, and detrimentally affected by other people's energy, no attempt should be made to help/heal others. To do so would have an unfavorable effect on their own health and energy signature.

We have to serve and heal our-self before we can truly be of service to others.

I have studied and qualified in many healing modalities: color and crystal therapy, meditation, yoga, exercise, Reconnective healing, aromatherapy, massage, reflexology and more. All of which, when applied, worked and made some distinct changes. But, apart from yoga, they weren't completely transformative and life changing. It wasn't until I researched the effects of diet and nutrition, and put into practice what I learnt, that an incredible transformation happened! All the pieces of the puzzle magically slotted together.

Five years ago, I thought I knew an awful lot about how to heal and balance the Empath, but I hadn't found complete balance within. It would have been hypocritical to write a book back then offering steps to find equilibrium, when I hadn't found them myself. Now I want to shout what I know from the rooftops and help the Empaths of the world discover for themselves how they too can make changes to their lives and find the protection and balance they need.

There are some who will argue that the Empath has the power within to protect themselves from the wayward energy of others (which is true) and they should not have to use any other protective shielding techniques other than applying their own divine source (which is also true). The problem we have is this: tapping into the incredible source of inner-power is nigh-on impossible to do until we have gained complete mastery over our trinity and addressed imbalances.

Imbalances

There are many levels of imbalance within the Empaths of the world. Some only have to make minor adjustments to see huge changes, others make huge changes only to see minor adjustments.

We are all different. No one should tell an Empath they are doing it wrong. Chances are, if an Empath is struggling in life, they have not yet found where their true imbalance lie or they may not yet be ready to face it.

On this journey we suffer, we learn and we grow. Although the suffering may be intolerable, once on the other side, we can see how it helped us grow and what we learnt from it. Imbalances may seem like cruel punishments, or ways to hold us back, but these obstacles offer opportunities in expansion.

In time, all Empaths come to accept their gift and all that comes with it. When ready, they will take the necessary steps to find balance and transmute or ride through the emotional storms they face. Until this balance is found, we will look at ways to navigate the myriad of energy debris Empaths face on a daily basis.

Shielding

No matter how great we feel as an Empath, we will always need to remain vigilante of negative energy and where it is coming from. A simple trip to the shops can mean we end up wearing someone else's energy for the rest of the day. Which isn't such a bad thing if it is positive and highly charged, but more often than not, it is the not-so-nice energy that clings to us and follows us home.

If you are one who finds being in public places, such as shopping malls and stadiums, unbearable to the point of avoiding them, there are some powerful techniques you can try for protection. I have found the best way to protect myself when out in public is by taking some preemptive measures, as well as having a few tactics to pull out of the bag, as and when needed.

Take a Friend

When an Empath is alone in people-congested areas they can soak up negatively charged energies no sooner than having stepped over the building's threshold. Being with another person (of whom you are energetically compatible) acts as a buffer and helps lessen the impact. It also serves as a pleasant distraction, taking your mind off what you are feeling. Chances are, after the shopping trip or outing, you may still feel drained or low in energy but your experience will have been a much more pleasant one.

If taking a friend or family member is not possible, finding a grounding technique, that works, and using it before going out is essential.

Power Poses

Holding a power pose for a couple of minutes prior to leaving home or entering an energy-hostile environment will serve in uplifting and expanding one's energy-field. This is opposed to how an Empath would normally go out into the world, wanting to be small and invisible.

Power poses are doable for everyone, no matter what their fitness level. Once performed you will notice a shift. This shift is a building of your energy-field which acts as an invisible shield against low-level energy.

A power pose is generally anything that opens the body, which in turn expands the energy-field. It can be as simple as opening up one's arms wide (so your body is in the shape of a cross). If you are familiar with yoga, a Starfish pose (standing with wide legs and arms) is ideal, as is a Warrior pose with open arms. Hold your pose for anything from thirty seconds to two minutes, whilst taking long slow breaths, through the nose, and focusing on your inner-power. Holding a gentle smile is further empowering.

Grounding Visualizations

These can be anything from visualizing roots, coming from your feet, grounding you to the earth, to mentally building a halo of white light around your body and expanding it with your breath.

Here is a quick one to try that can be done standing or seated:

Close your eyes and take some deep refreshing breaths. Take your awareness inside your body and feel any negative thoughts or energy quickly draining down into your feet. Imagine there are open stop taps on the soles of your feet allowing all the negative energy to drain out of your body, down into the center of the Earth, where it is cleansed and purified.

Next, picture roots coming from your feet, grounding you firmly. The energy of the Earth then rises up and surrounds you within an invisible, but powerful, force field. This is the Earth's protection and will keep you safe from any foreign energy when venturing into the world.

Music Therapy

Taking your music and earphones is an easy way to stay grounded and protected when out and about.

Listening to music you love creates an inner-expansion, it uplifts and creates a "bliss bubble" around you and enables you to glide through public-places seemingly unaffected. Make sure the music you choose is something you love or find emotionally uplifting and energizing.

Music is incredibly empowering to the Empath; it invokes prevailing sensations of love and happiness. The power of love is undeniable. Not much comes close, when wanting to create a cloak of protection, to the vibrations emitted by the energy of love.

It is best to get into the "music-zone" before entering a peopled place. This builds your invisible shield of protection, and prevents you from getting distracted.

Breath-Work

Breathing techniques can be done in a hurry or simply when one is feeling out of sorts. You may need to experiment with different techniques to find what works for you.

A technique, that proves to be popular with most people, is alternate nostril breathing. This method offers instant calm and can be used before, during or after spending time in people congested areas. It is a great way to calm your nerves and is relaxing but at the same time uplifting. The technique also balances your masculine and feminine energy.

Alternate Nostril Breathing: Sit comfortably with your back straight and eyes closed. Place the tip of the right thumb on the edge of the right nostril and the right ring finger hovering over the left nostril. Closing off the right nostril inhale through the left for a count of 3. Close the left nostril then exhale through the right for a count of 3, inhale through the right for a count of 3, close the right nostril and exhale through the left for a count of 3. This was 1 round. Practice as many rounds as needed.

It is normal when beginning breathing exercises to get a little dizzy, if this happens just resume normal breathing until it passes.

Salt

You may already know of the amazing healing properties of salt. It clears negative energies and also helps protect you from absorbing them. It has the power to draw out and dissolve negative energies from the emotional and physical body. This is especially helpful if your day involves interacting with others, where too often stressed or anxious energy is absorbed. Salt can also repel dark energy.

Use it before and after spending time in peopled places. Add it to you bath, use as a body scrub and include it in your diet.

Crystals:

The healing power of crystals has long been understood in many cultures, from Atlantis to ancient Egypt. It is known the ancients had crystal chambers that would be used to heal many an ailment by balancing the chakras with crystals.

Crystals offer protection from all sorts of negative energies. They also protect from electro-magnetic energy. Choose the ones you most resonate with and carry them with you when visiting people congested places.

Yoga

A short daily practice is a powerful protective tool for the Empath. Amongst many other amazing benefits, yoga helps balance and build your energy body, which is your invisible force field.

Singing

Yes, this may seem bonkers but it works! Sound affects us on many levels energetically. Yogis have used sound for thousands of years (chanting/song) because they know the power of it.

Singing raises your frequency, making negative energy bounce off. Try it when in peopled places or when you feel an incoming energy storm and see how it changes your vibration.

Avoid Caffeine

Any kind of stimulant leaves the Empath's energy-field wide open. Too much coffee, for example, can leave you vulnerable to other people's energy which is not good when spending time in public.

If you drink a lot of coffee, whilst in a peopled place, you may find your energy drain is much worse than what it would normally be.

Decaffeinated beverages are best consumed when spending time in crowds or busy places.

Essential Oils

The value of essential oils has been known for more than 6000 years. They are renowned not only for their amazing healing properties but for their ability to bring energetic balance back to the body and mind, and promote emotional wellbeing.

As well as their amazing healing qualities, essential oils can help build a powerful energetic shield and protect against residual energy. Use them in your body oils and face creams which will work in keeping you relaxed and empowered when out and about.

Part of what the Empath awakening is about is to become aware of how to stay protected from negative or excess energy. We are the ones who have to find out for ourselves that which works, and keep changing techniques as and when needed.

10

Empath Relationships

Volumes could be written about the relationships between an Empath and their family, friends, spouses and significant others.

The longer an Empath has been acquainted with another, the more impact they have on their energy. Knowing how to navigate relationships can serve in offering healthier and happier associations, which in turn creates a more joyful life.

Most Empaths, whether newly awakened or not, have difficulties within their relationships and they can cause more anguish, difficulties and upset than anything else in life, if we allow them.

A huge bugbear for the Empath is not understanding why others do not think or act in the same way. The fact that certain others seem blisteringly unaware of how their actions affect another, can cause hours of torment within the Empath's mind.

One way to prevent yourself from experiencing a mountain of unnecessary pain, in all your relationships, is to remember most don't come close to possessing the same level of empathy. The actions of others rarely reflect the same degree of consideration as your own, whether male or female, and, in truth, most (but not all) are incapable of showing the same kind of understanding. For the simple reason it is not in their genetic makeup.

It is difficult to comprehend how others seem so incapable of challenging their behavior. But we have to remember, when another shows a distinct lack of respect, or consideration, it does not mean their actions stem from cruel intent. Rather a lack of awareness. There is no point allowing the actions of those lacking empathic aptitude to cause needless suffering.

Sometimes, we really do need to stop taking things personally and keep reminding ourselves that those who act inconsiderately are just of a different mindset. When in balance, we have a choice of how we allow others' actions to affect us, and this is why it is so important to keep striving towards it.

An Empath can dwell for hours on what they consider to be a gross injustice by another, but the only person this hurts is the Empath. We have to make a choice. The second we decide we will no longer allow another's actions to control our emotions, and truly believe in this choice, is the second we find inner-peace. It may take us a while before we can make that declaration, but the moment we do a weight is lifted. Of course, it is always your choice if a person should remain in your life who behaves inconsiderately. As an Empath there are some who you may never be able to spend time with, without being thrown out of unity. We have to make peace with that. Also, some people's lack of consideration does not make for good, lifelong, acquaintances.

There is no denying it, some people do unthinkable things without so much as questioning themselves. But this type of behavior is a reflection of them and not you. If you were to confront another, about their unreasonable or inconsiderate conduct, it does not mean they will accept or understand your point of view. Sometimes, in those who have no moral compass, your words will either fall on deaf ears or activate a bitter resentment towards you. When this happens, they will not consider your comments, about their insensitive actions, instead you become the enemy and the one acting out-of-line. They will then do their utmost to reverse the situation, making you into the villain. Convincing themselves, and others, that it is you who is the "baddie". Because they have justified in their mind that you are the "outlaw", it makes it ok for them to verbally attack (which will be done behind your back) or take part in vengeful acts. Before we go any further I would like to say one word: Karma!

Karma exists! Everything you do will one day come back to you, good and bad. There is no getting away from it. We see evidence of karma at work every day; in our own lives and the lives of others. Even if you don't believe karma exists, it is a shrewd move to live your life as though it does. Call it insurance. When, or if, someone says cruel lies or does unthinkable things towards you, before you do anything, stop and breathe. The last thing you want is to get caught up in their karma. If you throw your energy into the situation, by going to war with the other person, this is exactly what will happen. I'm not saying lie down and allow them to trample all over you, but just back away with your emotional energy. If it involves a legal issue, let the solicitors deal with it. If they spread vicious rumors about you leave them to it.

People get wise to those who bitch, backstab and bicker. The truth always comes out in the end. Such is the way of karma. Stepping away from a situation, when another is intent on hurting you, with what they consider to be justifiable lies and actions, is not easy, but it will save you months of additional heartache and emotional stress. Trust in a higher power and know everything will work out.

When, or if, a friend, family member, partner or colleague repeatedly lies about you or takes unthinkably cruel actions, without questioning themselves, they are showing narcissistic traits.

The narcissist has no ethics and will not back down in a situation. Even when they know they are wrong, if they feel their standing has been challenged, they will fight tooth and nail to bring you down. If you express a truth about their behavior, they will tell a lie about you, to defame your character. If you defend yourself against their lie, they will simply tell more and more. And no, they won't question their actions.

The narcissist, or anyone with several narcissistic traits, will fight to protect their image regardless of what damage it does to others. In these situations, there is only one way to behave: back away and don't play. Yes, they will annoy, upset or enrage you but don't allow their actions to hurt you. You have a choice. Remember their behavior reflects on them, not you, and their karma will eventually come back their way. An Empath will rarely get anything out of a relationship of this ilk, other than upset, and they will be doing themselves a great service to disengage from the dynamic.

Toxic Relationships

Most Empaths have at least one toxic person in their life, who unwittingly activates waves of negative emotions.

It is normal for the toxic to talk disapprovingly of everyone and everything, and their low-level energy can drain one's happiness within minutes. These people, who may be a friend or family member, spew venom when they talk. It can feel like hot lava is being poured over the solar-plexus area just by spending time with them.

The solar-plexus, situated mid-stomach, is our seat of emotions, it is here where we feel the worse effects of negative energy. Even after trying every trick in the book, for self-protection, nothing seems to stop their venom seeping in. Toxic people often refuse to change their behavior.

There is a saying that if you want another to change their behavior towards you, then you need to change your behavior. This is certainly true, but only applies in certain situations. If, for example, you are always down in the dumps and constantly talk negatively, you will attract this type of energy back. If you act and talk positively, and exuberate a powerful vibration of gratitude, this is the energy returned. Acting positively has a powerful impact and will attract this type of behavior in others. But, sadly, it does not always work for the Empath.

Staying in a positive mindset, when around toxic people, may change their attitude towards you but it does not always protect from their residual negative energy.

Many Empaths find even when they approach a toxic person with super-high intentions and a warm positive outlook, they still get battered by their negative energy, during or after, time spent in their company. (Especially common in the out-of-balance.)

If someone's energy has a toxic vibration, which they refuse to work on, it will often impact the Empath, no matter how in balance they are.

What Causes Toxic Energy

Most people have deep insecurities and emotional anguish buried within, this does not mean they are toxic. Everyone has a history and holds pain from their past. The Empath senses this pain in another, but if it turns into blame it goes from being uncomfortable to intolerable for them. When emotional pain, and insecurities, are replaced with bitterness, anger or hatred they become toxic energy.

The toxic person may seem nice and friendly on the surface but deep down they are judging every move you make. They like to engage in the "he said, she said" discussions, and often stir up trouble between family and friends, pitting one person against another.

The toxic constantly complains, and are always angry or disappointed with you (even if they don't say it to your face). Deep down they are extremely unhappy and believe it is the responsibility of others (friends or family) to give them the happiness they deserve. They like to take, but give little in return; and only if it suits them. They refuse to accept or change their behavior, but expect the world to change for them, and they show traits of anger, bitterness, resentment, loathing and selfishness.

It is in the Empath's nature to want to help those who emit toxic energy and they may spend time with them in a bid to do this. But, as already discussed, we cannot help those who are unwilling to help themselves.

Here Are 5 Reactions Experienced with Toxic People:

1. **Being swamped by emotions, such as anger or bitterness**: These feelings can last up to 10 days. Depending on the traits they carry will depend on what you pick up and endure.

2. **Empath Fatigue**: Struggling to keep your eyes open, especially if they are venting. It is as if your body is trying to shut down and protect you from their negativity.

3. **Being out of sorts**: A range of strange feelings wash over you from being spaced out to nausea.

4. **Negative talk**: Finding yourself talking negatively about others, even though it is not a typical trait of yours. Overly toxic people can effortlessly lure the unvigilant Empath into their judgmental rants.

5. **Apathy**: Losing all zest, hope and optimism when spending any length of time with the toxic.

   The toxic person in your life will likely be a family member or lifelong friend. Because you have love for them, you have a natural fear of hurting or letting them go.

   Chances are, you have already tried helping them to see the error of their ways. Perhaps you shared what has helped you in life, or pointed them towards a motivational book or speaker. Sadly, the toxic one does not want to hear or listen, instead preferring to offload their negative opinions on others.

   The Empath would never want to hurt or cause unnecessary pain, to anyone, and it is for this reason they may keep in their lives, those who cause energetic disruptions and emotional pain. Yet, we must always remember to put the emotional health of oneself first. If you know a food or substance made you violently ill, or caused you to feel depressed, you would avoid it; the same should be applied to those who cause emotional turmoil.

We have a responsibility to keep our bodies and mental wellbeing strong and healthy. If another is causing us damage (all stress will eventually lead to illness), it is our duty to either confront said person or remove them from our life. This is not about wishing anyone harm or ill intent, and we do not need to get angry or resentful towards them. It is about doing what is best for the trinity of mind, body and spirit, and letting them go with love.

Those who violate you with cruel intentions and negative energy are causing your body harm. They may not be punching you with a fist or stabbing you with a knife, but their energy can cause considerable damage to your mental and emotional wellbeing. The effects of which can last for years. People don't think twice about staying away from people who are violent, but we should also display the same level of trepidation with those who have a destructive energy and cruel intentions.

When I talk about staying away from those with toxic energy, I am not talking about having one's ego dented by another's random disrespect. We all have people who offend, hurt or make us angry by their lack of understanding, at some point. And we in turn will no doubt do the same to others. The issue is about those toxic friends, or family members, who repetitively bring you down and do immense energetic damage.

The sad truth is the toxic person is not happy inside, but the only person who can change that is them. If they are unwilling to listen and accept help, in changing their ways, there is nothing you can do to help.

Navigating relationships is difficult, because most people will invoke conflict within the Empath at some time. The point will come when one has to decide if it is causing more harm than good.

Here are some questions to ask yourself that may help you decide:

- Am I taking anything from this relationship?
- Does spending time with her make me happy?
- Do I dread being in his presence?
- When was the last time I enjoyed being in her company?
- Do we have any of the same interests?

- Is it a one-sided friendship, with me fitting in with his needs?
- Does this relationship affect my emotional health?
- Do I feel ill, emotionally drained or intense negative emotions after being with her?
- Am I being used as an emotional dumping ground?
- Does he have a lot of negative thoughts or anger towards me?
- Am I learning anything from spending time with her?
- Is being in this relationship making me grow spiritually, emotionally or other?
- Is this relationship beneficial to either of us?
- Has she become dependent upon me?
- What are my real reasons for staying in this relationship?

Magic Mirror

From my experience there are many reasons we encounter toxic people in our lives. One of the most common being the magic mirror. Certain experiences, or encounters, with others act as a mirror and show us weaknesses or issues we need to resolve within ourselves.

You may already have seen a pattern of repetitive behavior in family and friends towards you. For example: others may act overly needy with you or, going to the other end of the spectrum, they may not be there for you, especially when you need them. If you have noticed the actions of others following a trend, it is not happening by chance. When anything repeats itself in life, it happens so you can learn something from it.

Difficult relationships are often the universe's way of highlighting issues we are refusing to see in ourselves. Issues we need to work on. We all learn from experiences and situations presented to us in life. When we allow ourselves to see them for what they are, we can then take the lesson.

Some toxic people show up in our lives to press our buttons, some to make us aware of our behavior that needs addressing, and some genuinely need our guidance. Beyond that, we have to consider the lesson we may need to learn from a toxic relationship is about having the courage to let it go.

We learn a lot from bad people and bad experiences, but we don't need to keep on experiencing them over and over. It does not help them or us. Once we have learnt from an experience, we do not need to re-learn it.

Repetitive, painful emotions will eventually become illness. If anyone leaves a dark energetic imprint on us, simply by being in their presence, they will cause harm.

We need to recognize when it is time to let go. This is not about wishing them ill intent; it is about protecting oneself. We can still love those we let go and be grateful for all they have taught us in life. And, in the long-run, both parties will benefit.

When it is a close family member, such as parent or sibling, cutting the chord that binds you is, in some cases, difficult to do and only done as a last resort. If you have been honest in explaining how their toxic behavior affects you, how it hurts and brings you down, and they still do nothing to change, then they are making the decision they no longer want you in their life.

Just like some people are addicted to bad habits that destroy relationships, some people are addicted to negativity (although they would argue against that) and are not willing to change.

Any type of addiction, whether it be to drugs, alcohol, gambling or food, creates a selfish, self-centered demeanor. Addicts have to be willing to give up their addiction before they can change their behavior.

Releasing toxic people is also not about ditching those in the throes of an emotional shift. Anyone going through a transitional stage in life, such as a mid-life crisis, the moody teen years, a divorce, bereavement or any type of loss, are in pain and will often exhibit poor behavior.

Those who are suffering will act out of character and often need a lot of support (if even from a distance) and guidance. The difference is, those in crisis are often willing to make changes to help ease their pain and they listen to suggestions. Toxic people refuse to address their behaviors, and they won't listen or make any changes (they want others to change for them).

People's behaviors are always affected during difficult times; often becoming darker and out-of-character. We all go through them. There may be periods when we too emit a dark sticky energy and are difficult to be around, but this should, hopefully, only be transitional stage and not a permanent stopover in toxic-land.

Navigating Relationships

For the Empath, relationships can prove to be a complicated area of life. But also very rewarding when one has found a compatible mate, who very likely won't be an Empath. That is not to say Empath relationships don't happen or work. They do and can. But when two highly Sensitive people become coupled it can cause a clash of personality and energy.

We might assume that two Empaths would be a match made in heaven. But, more often than not, this is not the case. It works like a mirror, each reflecting back comparable insecurities or pains. When the energy signature of two people is too similar it can often act as a repellant. That said, you will find some Empaths who encompass very different attributes and traits and in these cases relationships often work.

The law of attraction states that like energy attracts like energy. But, when it comes to relationships, this law becomes complicated. Our relationships don't happen by accident. Our higher-self will guide us towards those we are meant to be with and those who we can learn from. Sometimes it will be a complete opposite.

To create balance and gain knowledge, we will often choose, in mates, those who carry strengths where we have weakness and vice versa. If we lack confidence, we may choose a partner who exuberates it, if we lack willpower we may be drawn to one who has stacks, and if we are timid and shy we may pick a partner who is loud and brash. As I said, nothing happens by accident. Even bad relationships have a higher purpose. We discover much by experiencing the many ups and downs of any type of relationship.

The Highs and Lows

Empaths are a greatly misunderstood breed. Their quiet demeanor is often mistakenly interpreted as standoffish behavior. Because they may appear aloof and disconnected, to a new or prospective partner, it can be taken as a rejection. It may take a while for their detachment, and need for time alone, not to be taken personally.

When one is romantically connected to another, it can make the energetic connection complicated. Reading someone, who holds no emotional ties, normally comes quite easily for the Empath. But when there is a strong emotional bind, it often distorts one's ability to read energies clearly. This can lead to confusion and frustration.

An Empath may not speak a lot about their true feelings, but when they do, they will try to keep it honest. Not everyone is inclined to be as honest as an Empath; especially those who have either grown-up or worked in an environment where lying is "quietly" seen as acceptable (it is surprising how often this is the case). This causes concern for the Empath because they feel the energy of a lie, but not always what the lie is. In some cases, this can lead to paranoia which in turn leads to accusations and arguments

There will always be situations where people tell white lies to avoid getting into trouble and sometimes they are told to prevent unnecessary hurt being caused. But most "little fibs" are told when someone is protecting themselves and not considering how their words or actions will affect others.

All lies feel the same, for the Empath, whatever the intention behind them. Untruths cause hurt and are often the footings on which resentments are built.

As a Sensitive, we have to learn to allow others to have their minor dishonesties without allowing them to bring us down. If someone is a good person, the Empath will feel it and this is what we should focus on when it comes to relationships. We all make mistakes and we should be allowed to make them.

What I said earlier, about others not having the same empathic capacity, is relevant for all Empath relationships. We need to remember not everyone has an Empath's consideration or nose for honesty. But a great thing to know is: when it comes to long-term relationships, our strongest traits rub off on others. Traits like honesty and consideration also develop in those who we share our lives with (as does the intolerance to negative energy). Live alike, grow alike.

A whole book could be dedicated to the relationship highs and lows of an Empath and how to handle each and every situation. But, in brief, it's safe to say the best way to be in any relationship is honest (unless the truth will cause unnecessary pain) and never be afraid to show your True-Self.

The Out-of-Balance Empath

A point all Empaths have to contemplate, when considering the behavior of others in any relationship, is how out-of-balance we are. The reason I say this is because when imbalanced the emotional pain we experience can border on being irrational.

Irrational behavior will result in us making a mountain out of a molehill. Too often it is unsettled body chemistry responsible for flighty moods and hypersensitivity. Unstable hormones will ignite emotional instability and they will interfere with how we observe and interpret a situation. Any female, who has experienced a monthly menstrual cycle, can vouch for this.

Hormones are behind many distresses and overreactions. A slight shift in the correct levels of any one of our hormones affects our moods, making the Empath even more sensitive than normal (in both male and females).

If those in your life frequently remark that you are overreacting to situations, it might be time to question your hormonal imbalances.

If you want to learn more about how certain hormonal imbalances are caused and how they can affect the chakras and energy body, see my book: 7 Secrets of the Sensitive.

11

At the Helm

Life is a series of experiences; linked together like the spots on a child's dot-to-dot puzzle. The more dots we connect the clearer our life-picture becomes.

Most are unaware that the seemingly random occurrences, of daily life, are in any way pivotal to the course of their destiny. A chance meeting ten years ago may be the precursor for an incredible job offer tomorrow, a difficult situation endured in our teens could help us overcome an incident in our forties and a book read today may play a huge part in transforming our future path.

Part of the Empath awakening is about becoming aware of these amazing synchronicities.

Our conscious mind is kept so busy, making sense of life's conundrums, that it keeps us from connecting the dots on our cosmic mystery puzzle, and prevents us from seeing just how amazing our lives really are.

The majority of Empaths work hard trying to figure out life. We ponder our purpose and wonder where we are supposed to fit into this crazy old world. Sadly, much of our present life is missed when our mind either races ahead or hangs out in the problems from our past.

Our thoughts keep our mind busy, either making plans for approaching events or contemplating what will bring most happiness. It is as though our happiness lies in tomorrow's achievements or is put on hold for some day in the future... That future day does not exist. The only day we can be happy is today.

It's funny how we tell ourselves our future plans will bring us our well-deserved and long overdue happiness, without realizing just how many of our goals we have already achieved. Most of which, came and went without being noticed or celebrated, because our minds had already skipped off to make more plans. If our goals were recognized but did not bring the feelings of joy or completion we expected, we then pin our hopes on the next big dream.

Waiting for that elusive day, when our happiness and sense of purpose is supposed to arrive, is like waiting for old age. We are just wishing our life away.

Happiness is already within; we just need to know how to access it. And, until we shake it and wake it up, nothing we do, achieve or gain will bring anything more than a short-lived euphoria.

You have already found your chosen path. You are walking it, working on it and learning from it every day. Each step revealing more of the bigger picture.

Your true path started the moment you took your first gasp of air and has been unfolding ever since. All the events and achievements in your life, both good and bad, have played a part in your dot-to-dot picture, and it is up to each of us to keep this picture unfolding. By the time we leave this body, the idea is to have completed our chosen voyage (or we just come back to finish it).

Roadblocks

Sometimes life throws obstacles, or roadblocks, our way. These obstacles may seem like cruel ways to keep us from our dreams and happiness, but this is often not the case. Roadblocks may stop us from travelling our desired or chosen routes in life, but it is always for a reason. They are seen through sickness, redundancy, not getting the dream job, depression, loss of money and social status, non-starting projects and many more. They happen abruptly, taking us off our current journey and bringing normal life to a halt.

When life suddenly stops, or shifts course, it always has a purpose. We may be meant for a new direction, or have more to learn at this current stage of life to prepare us for our future.

Wanting to rush towards our goals, and have it all today, is normal. But when anything turns up too easily we get no real sense of accomplishment or achievement.

When our dreams take longer to unfold, we are being given an opportunity to enjoy the journey, whilst preparing for their arrival.

Sadly, many people give up on their visions because their goals don't arrive quick enough, or they've had enough of the roadblocks; looking elsewhere for what they believe will bring happiness or completion.

This just leaves a trail of half-finished ambitions and disappointments. It is one thing seeing a project through, before moving onto the next, but to never experience completion is a crime against yourself.

When encountering roadblocks, it may seem like an unfair punishment, but this comes down to our perspective. In the bigger scheme of things, it is just a detour presented as a way to find our-self on life's journey.

This detour may involve a long and winding scenic-route, which also happens to be an uncomfortable, seemingly never-ending, bumpy road. But again, this is down to our perspective. We have a choice: we can get wrapped up in the inconvenience and discomfort of the long "scenic-route", focusing only on that, or we can concentrate on the ever-changing landscape as it passes and be grateful for being given a chance to change, slow down and enjoy the journey.

A roadblock may also be an opportunity to evaluate your life and what you are doing. Are you trailing a path you do not believe in? are you chasing money instead of passion? or are you following someone else's recipe for life success? We are unique and our journey should reflect this.

Empaths have powerful inner-guidance that will lead us towards our true path, if only we allow ourselves to hear it.

We need to remember to be grateful and enjoy each moment of the journey. We are often so focused on where we are going that we miss the present and all the magical moments it offers. It is vital to be grateful for every experience along the way, good and bad, they both teach us more than we could ever know.

I learnt more from having bad experiences than I have from the good. How we conduct our-self when we go through challenging times, and come out the other side, is a true testimony to our spirit. Everything is in divine order.

Thoughts about a situation make it unbearable and not the situation itself.

Every challenge we endured in the past has always worked out. We are given nothing we cannot handle. We can become so caught up in the thought of arriving at our destination, that we miss most of the journey.

Everything presented to us in life is a gift and is something we can learn from, good or bad, if only we allow ourselves to see it.

Yes, the path of the Sensitive one is a challenging path to walk. It is strenuous, painful, overly emotional and can be lonely, but it is also enlightening, invigorating and electrically charged and, when we allow ourselves to see it: absolutely fantastic!

When it comes staying the course of our journey there are simple some ways of being that will help keep you in the right frame of mind and keep your inner-drive strong:

Laughter

As grown-ups we spend too much time being solemn and serious, and too little time having fun (especially in the current times). Do you remember the last time you had a proper belly-laugh?

'You don't stop playing because you grow old; you grow old because you stop playing!'

We hear children laugh all the time. Most of them don't know how to take life seriously, it's all about play and fun. We should all strive to stay childlike.

To see the world in wonder and above all have fun and laugh. Anything that makes us laugh will make our spirits soar. It really is a therapy.

Watch a film or comedy sitcom that makes you laugh, spend time with those who can't take life seriously, read amusing books, get into mischief, partake in fun past-times or go and watch a comedian. Look for what makes you laugh and allow yourself to giggle. Once you start laughing it becomes infectious and you start searching out forms of amusement.

When you laugh you literally feel your body vibrate and tingle. Laughing shakes off negative energy and puts you in positive space.

Stay Positive

Keeping a positive mindset will help you remain happy and give you more reasons to laugh. We have a choice of how we feel (when we are in balance) and by choosing positivity you not only build up self-confidence and a powerful outlook on life, but you will see those around you become more positive.

When you adopt a positive attitude your frequency rises. Having the attitude of, 'you can and will' empowers you and instills drive and determination.

The biggest reason people are knocked out of their positive place is because of roadblocks. Things such as: receiving criticism, taking on negativity, non-starting-projects, things not unfolding fast enough and being out-of-balance are often responsible. If you change your perspective on why these setbacks occur, it is a game changer. Holding onto pain serves no one.

Whatever life throws at you, take it in your stride and know it serves a higher purpose.

If you have been knocked out of your positive mindset, for one reason or another, simply bring your awareness back to positivity. Keep reminding yourself that everything happens for a reason and stay intent on living this life to the full with an open positive mind.

When you give the world positivity, you will receive positivity back. Like attracts like. Being positive releases a true sense of gratitude and this in itself is liberating.

Feel Gratitude

Regularly expressing gratitude sends a message out into the universe and the universe responds by giving you more to be grateful for. If you make this a daily practice your body will seek out experiences and reasons to be grateful. This has the effect of bringing you more happiness and success.

We really should express gratitude for everything we have in life and every experience, both good and bad. Being grateful for bad experiences, when we are going through them, is no easy task, but believing everything is or will be okay and being grateful for that is doable. When we come through the other side of any dark or challenging times, we will always find an amazing lesson from the experience. If we look for the good in everything we will find it.

One way we can find ways to be grateful is by having a gratitude journal. If you have read any of my books you will know I am a big fan of journaling.

Journals are a great place to offload or manifest your dreamlife. Keeping a gratitude diary is perfect way to see all the blessings you have in your life and be grateful for them.

Expressing gratitude opens your heart like nothing else and when your heart opens, love pours in and life opens to a new chapter.

Express Love Through an Open Heart

All you need is love. By making changes to your life, and finding balance as an Empath, your heart center opens and you feel an enormous shift in your energy. When your heart opens, it comes with an immense sense of love and gratitude for everything. The way you view your world shifts and much of the fear you may once have carried dissolves.

The heart's opening generally happens in small stages. Many of us have been experiencing profound moments of bliss lately. This bliss is triggered by the opening of our heart. It is a powerful sense of love, and an energy we want to project out into the world. This energy will help elevate the vibration of our planet.

How we behave, act and feel is so important now. Not just to us, but to everyone. What we feel, we project out into the world and when taken off center, our mood shifts to a lower vibration and our awareness is compromised. We need to remain vigilante of keeping our heart open and we can do this by expressing love.

Love and appreciation opens us up like nothing else. When our heart center opens, like a lotus flower, it offers us a protection to which little else can compare. It enforces our energy-field, protecting us from the emotional energy of others, and strengthens our chakras. As you would imagine, this an absolute gift for all Empaths.

It is difficult for anyone, not just the Empaths, to have an open heart when one is out-of-balance. But you should now have an idea what to do to find balance. Whether you choose to find it is entirely up to you. If you ignore your inner-promptings, to make changes, your life will become more and more uncomfortable until one day you will have to step up and make the necessary changes.

The easy path in life never turns out to be easy, it just takes you the long way round.

Sail Away

We are at the helm of our own ships. These ships can take us anywhere we want to go. If we want to stay moored in the harbor and not venture into unfamiliar territory, then that is our choice. But, by staying put, we will miss out on all the amazing experiences the journey offers.

When out on the vast ocean, steering our ship through calm and rough seas, riding the choppy waves and surfing the smooth, navigating storms and sailing through still waters, we have many incredible, life-changing experiences. We become stronger, wiser and more grateful.

Having traversed the storms and come through the other side, we come to appreciate life, and see how everything has purpose and meaning. We know there will be storms ahead, but we also know they too will pass.

When we choose the safe option of staying in harbor, we only see the surrounding landscape and have a limited outlook on life. And because we have never ventured out into the world, we fear what might be beyond the confines of this safe haven. It is this fear that typically keeps us securely anchored.

Some may stay in harbor, others will sail to one or two ports and get no further. As an Empath, we have the opportunity to voyage the Seven Seas and experience a life few others will encounter. But unless we set sail, and keep moving forward, we will miss out on so many opportunities and the true pinnacle of our journey may never be experienced. We get out of life what we put in.

'Twenty years from now you will be more disappointed by the things that you didn't do than by the ones you did do. So throw off the

bowlines. Sail away from the safe harbor.
Catch the trade winds in your sails. Explore.
Dream. Discover.' – Mark Twain

By striving to improve and constantly moving forward, you will receive magnificent rewards in life. Find your passion and follow your truth! We are in these bodies for such a short time we need to be reminded not to miss a moment.

Remember your journey is happening for you today and every day, be part of it and enjoy because we do not know when it will end.

The Empath awakening is your call to start making changes, uncover where your imbalances lie, make changes and see your truth and happiness unfold.

Be the change, see the change, reclaim your power and live the life you were born to live!

Other Books

for Empaths

by Diane Kathrine

17034533R00096

Printed in Poland
by Amazon Fulfillment
Poland Sp. z o.o., Wrocław